MW00909693

The Kitchen Dance
A New Take on Kosher Cooking

ELANA MILSTEIN AND ROB YUNICH

May you have as much fun in the kitchen as we did.

Rob
and Elana

The Kitchen Dance: A New Take on Kosher Cooking

Copyright © 2009 Elana Milstein and Rob Yunich. All rights reserved. No part of this book may be reproduced or retransmitted in any form or by any means without the written permission of the publisher.

Published by Wheatmark®

610 East Delano Street, Suite 104

Tucson, Arizona 85705 U.S.A.

www.wheatmark.com

International Standard Book Number: 978-1-60494-324-5

Library of Congress Control Number: 2009935310

To all those who inspired us, taught us, supported us, cooked for us, tasted our food, and helped us along the path toward publishing this book: we couldn't have done it without you!

Acknowledgments

It's impossible to list everybody who has eaten at our house, helped us, or given us an idea without omitting somebody. Therefore, we'd like to begin with an expansive thank-you to all of our family, friends, friends who might as well be blood relatives, and anybody else who has supported us along the way.

A special bit of gratitude goes to:

* Our parents—Charna and Yaakov Milstein, Libby Saypol, and Bob and Joanne Yunich—who have made an indelible impact on our lives and supported us through thick and thin.

* Our favorite siblings, Gershona and Ron Fein, for giving us ideas and, well, just for being yourselves.

* Rob's paternal grandmother, Beverly Yunich (our only living grandparent), who is a big part of our lives.

* Our deceased grandparents, who loved us and continue to inspire us.

* Mat Tonti, for designing the "Kitchen Dance" logo found on the apron on the front cover.

* Congregation Olam Tikvah and Gesher Jewish Day School, for being the center of our Jewish lives.

* And last, but certainly not least, the team at Wheatmark, especially Kat Gautreaux and Grael Norton, who helped us publish this book and worked with us during a very rewarding and detailed process.

Contents

VEGETARIAN MAIN DISHES

MEAT MAIN DISHES

DESSERTS

Introduction

Welcome to a new adventure for kosher and vegetarian cooks. The recipes and tips within these pages will help you, whether you're part of the younger, working crowd, the older, retired community, or anywhere in between. Whether you're single, in a relationship, or married, this book is for you.

The book earns its name from many people's struggle to keep a kosher home in tight quarters. As the cover drawing illustrates, it's often difficult to "dance" around somebody else in the kitchen while preparing a meal, all while sticking to recipes and making sure everything is cooked properly. If you've been facing this struggle for years and never seemed to find a cookbook that understood your quandary, worry no more. Whether you need to make dinner after a long day at the office or you want to make a special meal in a flash, this is a cookbook that feels your pain.

We've both been cooking since we were young. Elana started by making tahina with her Israeli father (the recipe is on p. 33), while Rob began preparing dinner for his family when he was a teenager. In 2002, shortly after meeting on a softball team, Rob invited Elana over to his very small apartment for dinner and, almost magically, started doing the "kitchen dance." (A recipe inspired by that first dinner can be found on p. 72.) That experience led to many more successful meals in the kitchen and, in many ways, to our marriage in 2004.

For many years now, we've been "dancing" around each other in the kitchen, inviting people to our home, and trying to make a special dinner every night of the week. We hope that, no matter what your relationship status might be, we can help make your eating experience more special.

Many of the recipes in this book are very easy to make and don't require any culinary degree. (We certainly don't have one.) Most can be made pretty quickly, but some do take a bit longer and require a little more work. Our hope is that you make our recipes part of your repertoire.

All of the recipes in this book are kosher, and a vast majority of them also are vegetarian. That means there is no mixing of meat and milk, and there is no use of non-kosher animals (most noticeably pork). You can read more about the rules of kashrut, and find a list of reliable kosher symbols that appear on packages, at http://kosherfood.about.com.

Throughout the book, icons at the top of every recipe help you decipher how the dishes are designated (look for the saucepan): pareve, dairy, or meat. This also will help those who are lactose intolerant or have food allergies. If a recipe is marked pareve, there is no milk or meat in it at all.

We've included some sample menus on p. 11, and we have noted many recipes that are suitable for Passover with little or no change.

If you're a vegetarian, Jewish or not, you'll have plenty of recipes from which to choose. In fact, other than those in chapter 4 (and the chicken soup recipe), every recipe in this book will fit your lifestyle.

Thanks for joining us on this culinary adventure. Please feel free to email us and share your feedback. We look forward to hearing from you!

Rob and Elana

info@thekitchendance.com

How to Do the Kitchen Dance

Size matters when it comes to kitchens. Small spaces aren't always conducive to one person making a meal, let alone two or more people. In our first kitchen, we could practically touch all three walls at the same time (the fourth side was open). The room clearly was not designed by people who liked to entertain.

While we can't give you "chemistry" lessons, we hope that these tips will help your culinary experience in contained quarters:

* **Read the entire recipe first**. Check all the steps in a recipe before getting started. Some dishes involve letting a vegetable (such as eggplant) sit for 60 to 90 minutes before it can be used. This also will give you time to plan your menu and decide who's going to do what, which leads us to ...

* **Split up the duties for each recipe**. Many dishes in this book involve chopping several vegetables, warming up a cooking vessel, or other preparatory tasks. Divide and conquer, and you'll speed up the process while spending quality time together.

* **Make different dishes simultaneously, side by side**. If a meal has several components, each person should take charge of one. Have one person make the soup, while somebody else crafts the cake.

* **Don't repeat actions**. If an ingredient (or several) is needed for multiple dishes, have one person do the work for everybody. There's no reason for two people to chop onions when one person can complete the task.

* **Learn each other's movements by giving vocal clues**. For example, say "behind" if you're about to walk behind someone, or "watch your head" if you're opening a cabinet. It might seem like a no-brainer, but these little things go a long way toward developing kitchen chemistry.

* **Have fun!** Cooking should be enjoyable. Don't be afraid to make mistakes or improvise. Some of our best recipes came from adjusting midcourse, and we hope you can say the same before too long.

How to Be Ready

As with any trade, cooking requires having the right tools on hand—most importantly, food and equipment. We don't expect you to have everything listed below in your kitchen at all times; acquiring things incrementally is the right approach. However, we wanted you to have one place to look when you're ready to start buying.

PANTRY ITEMS ON HAND:

Oil (olive, vegetable, and sesame)
Vinegar (rice, red wine, and balsamic)
Honey
Teriyaki sauce
Low-sodium soy
Roasted red peppers in a jar
Sloppy joe sauce
Rice (jasmine and arborio)
Pasta (various cuts, spaghetti)
Rice noodles
Dried lentils
Canned tuna packed in water
Panko (Japanese) bread crumbs
Matzah meal
Pistachio nuts, shelled
Falafel mix
Boxes of stock (beef, vegetable, or chicken)
Canned tomato paste
Canned plain tomato sauce
Canned crushed tomatoes
Canned diced tomatoes
Canned beans (cannellini, black, red kidney, light kidney, pinto)
Canned corn, no salt added
Whole berry/jellied cranberry sauce
Tahina (seasoned sesame paste)
Preserves (strawberry, raspberry, or apricot)
Taco/fajita seasoning
Bottled barbecue sauce

Italian salad seasoning packets
Onion soup mix (dried, reduced sodium)

PAPER PRODUCTS:

Parchment or wax paper
Aluminum foil
Plastic wrap
Paper towels
Food storage bags (quart and gallon sizes)
Toothpicks
Napkins
Fancy paper plates (for large dinner parties)
Fancy paper cups (for large dinner parties)
Plastic utensils

REFRIGERATED ITEMS:

Ketchup
Yellow mustard
Mayonnaise
Bottles of lemon and lime juice
Unsalted stick margarine
Soy milk, nonfat plain
Eggs
Celery
Carrots (baby, shredded, whole)
Lettuce
Cheese (Parmesan, cheddar, mozzarella)
Sour cream (light, pareve)
Bell peppers (red, yellow, green, orange)
Mushrooms (portabella, crimini, white, button)
Cucumbers
Leeks
Green onions
Fruit (apples, oranges, grapes, strawberries, pineapple)
Salad dressing (pareve is best)

NONREFRIGERATED ITEMS:

Nonstick cooking spray (vegetable or olive oil flavor)
Onions (red, yellow, white, Vidalia)

Potatoes (red, Yukon gold, russet)
Fresh lemons and/or limes
Garlic

FROZEN ITEMS:

Corn
Broccoli
Asparagus
Chopped spinach
Vegetable mixes
Puff pastry

BAKING ITEMS ON HAND:

Unbleached all-purpose flour
Granulated white sugar
Brown sugar
Confectioners' sugar
Cornmeal
Oats (old fashioned, quick cooking)
Yellow cake mix
Instant pudding (pistachio, vanilla)
Cocoa powder
Baking powder
Baking soda
Vanilla extract
Baking spray that contains flour
Chocolate chips (pareve, semisweet)
Solid vegetable shortening
Chocolate-flavored syrup (pareve is best)

BASIC COOKING EQUIPMENT:

Mixing bowls of various sizes
8–10 quart stockpot
Sauté pans/skillets (8, 10, or 12 inches)
Covered saucepans (1-, 2-, 3-, or 4-quart sizes)
Baking sheets
Cutting boards (including one designated solely for raw meats)
Spatulas
Mixing spoons

Slotted spoons
Whisks
Tongs
Ladles
Knives (chef, paring, utility, etc.)
Measuring cups and spoons for dry ingredients
Glass measuring cups for liquids
Oven-safe glass baking dishes
9 × 13 inch nonstick baking pan
8 × 8 (or 9 × 9) inch nonstick baking pan
Colander/strainer
Vegetable peeler

OTHER EQUIPMENT:

Slow cooker
Hand mixer
Food processor
Electric juicer
Mandolin slicer
Timer
Manual can opener
Box grater
Lemon squeezer
Meat thermometer
Refrigerator thermometer
Pot holders/oven mitts
Bulb baster
Metal potato masher
Apron

BAKING EQUIPMENT:

Rolling pin (French is preferred)
Cookie cutters of various shapes and sizes
Bundt pans of various sizes and shapes
Offset spatula for frosting cakes, etc.
Cooling racks
Pastry brush (rubber is preferred)

Platters
Bowls
Forks
Spoons
Cake slicer/server
Trivets
Linen tablecloths

DRIED/GROUND HERBS AND SPICES:

Kosher salt
Black pepper
Rosemary leaves
Oregano
Paprika
Garlic powder
Onion powder
Bay leaves
Ground cinnamon
Ground cumin
Thyme leaves
Italian seasoning
Chili powder
Saffron

FRESH HERBS:

Dill
Rosemary
Thyme
Parsley
Basil

Sample Menus

As you start to cook more frequently, you'll be able to craft your own menus. Here are some of our favorites to help you out.

Shabbat

Homemade Chicken Soup, p. 17
Pistachio Chicken, p. 93
Green Salad (bagged or freshly made)
Jasmine Rice Pilaf, p. 39
Pistachio Chocolate Cake, p. 121

Sukkot

Slow Cooker Beef Stew, p. 111, or Elana's Famous Vegetarian Chili, p. 55
Corn Bread, p. 47
Israeli Salad, p. 31
Baked Apple Crisp, p. 125

Shavuot

Vegetable Minestrone Soup, p. 24
Crustless Quiche, p. 75
Milstein Family Fruit Salad, p. 133
Sin Cake, p. 127

Rosh Hashanah

Panko Encrusted Honey Mustard Chicken, p. 91
Grandma Marian's Meatballs, p. 113
Potato Kugel, p. 43
Green Salad (bagged or freshly made)
Grandma Marian's Apple Cake, p. 124

Passover Seder

Potato and Leek Soup, p. 21
Brisket, p. 115
Green Salad (bagged or freshly made)
Farfel Stuffing, p. 45
Passover Jam Bars, p. 136

Other Tips

It's important to know a few things about food safety before you get started. As noted in the equipment section, you should buy a meat thermometer and, if possible, also get a thermometer for your refrigerator and oven. When cooking meat, remember that its internal temperature needs to be at a safe level for eating: red meat should be at least 145 degrees, ground beef or turkey 160 degrees, and poultry 165 degrees. (Check out http://www.foodsafety.gov for more information.)

After you've handled raw meat or poultry, remember to wash your hands and any surfaces or cutting boards thoroughly with lots of soap. It would be ideal to designate a cutting board to use only for raw meat or poultry. And, while we're on that subject, do not refreeze any raw chicken or beef. If you've frozen it once after getting back from the store, you *must* cook it after the first time you thaw it.

Thoroughly wash and dry all fruits and vegetables before you use them. And just like with raw meat or poultry, try to designate a cutting board to use just for cutting fruits and vegetables.

Finally, hand shredding cheese is a much better solution than buying pre-shredded cheese. Not only do you save money, but the cheese tastes better because you don't have to put up with additives used to keep the cheese from caking. It might take a few extra minutes, but it is well worth it! And when you get to the end of the cheese block, either cut it up or just eat it as a snack.

Soups
and
Salads

Homemade Chicken Soup

Chicken soup has been called the Jewish penicillin for many years, and for good reason. It's so good that it has mystical powers to heal illness or make you feel better after a bad day. It's also been known as a building block for a happy marriage.

Meat

 INGREDIENTS:

16 cups water
1 chicken, cut up (about 3 pounds)
3 yellow onions, sliced in half (skin removed)
5–6 whole carrots, peeled, with ends removed
4 celery stalks, ends removed
1 handful fresh dill, chopped fine
1 chicken flavored bouillon cube
Salt, to taste
Ground black pepper, to taste

 DIRECTIONS:

Add water, chicken pieces, onions, carrots, celery, and dill to an 8-quart stockpot. Add 2 teaspoons each of salt and pepper (you will be adding more seasoning later).

Bring the chicken and vegetables to a boil. Skim any chicken fat that accumulates on top.

Taste for flavor. Add a pinch or two more salt or ground black pepper if needed. Cover the pot and reduce the heat to low. Simmer for 1 hour.

Taste again, and add seasoning as needed. Add the bouillon cube. Simmer for another hour, until the chicken is falling off the bone.

Remove the chicken from the soup and take the meat off the bone, throwing away the skin. Set aside.

Remove all the other vegetables and cut them up. Make sure to remove all bones from the soup.

Return the cut-up chicken and vegetables to the soup. It is now ready to serve.

Makes 12 generous servings.

Passover Friendly

The Easiest Vegetable Soup You'll Ever Make

Eight days after we were married, we (amazingly) hosted a large seder at our very small apartment. We needed something for our vegetarian cousin, so we cooked up this easy-to-make dish that wowed even the biggest meat lovers in the crowd.

Pareve

 INGREDIENTS:

4 tablespoons extra-virgin olive oil
5 teaspoons kosher salt, divided
2 medium white or yellow onions, diced
1 bunch green onions, finely chopped (both white and green parts)
3 medium russet potatoes, cubed
2 medium red bell peppers, diced
10 ounces crimini mushrooms, finely chopped
1 (12-ounce) bag petite carrots, chopped (or fresh carrot chips)
3–4 stalks celery, finely chopped
4–6 cloves garlic, minced
3 bay leaves
8 cups vegetable stock

 DIRECTIONS:

Pour 1 teaspoon of the oil into a stockpot over high heat. When you see the oil shimmering, put in the white or yellow onions and the first round of salt, and reduce the heat to medium. Sauté for 5 minutes.

Add the green onions and cook for another 5 minutes.

Add the potatoes and another teaspoon of salt. Sauté the potatoes for about 5 minutes.

Add the bell peppers and mushrooms along with another teaspoon of salt. Continually mix the vegetables for 5 minutes.

Add the carrots, celery, and garlic along with another teaspoon of salt. Sauté for another 5 minutes to let the flavors combine.

Add the bay leaves and vegetable stock.

Cover and cook for about 45 minutes, or until all the vegetables are soft. Remove the bay leaves before serving.

Makes 12 generous servings.

PASSOVER FRIENDLY TIP:

If you can't find vegetable stock in a carton, make some using vegetable powder and water.

Potato and Leek Soup

The potatoes act as a natural thickener and turn this dish into a stew-like treat perfect for Sukkot, Passover, or an average Wednesday night.

Pareve

 INGREDIENTS:

16 cups water
12 tablespoons vegetable soup powder
3 large leeks, prepared as described below
2 tablespoons extra-virgin olive oil
2 tablespoons kosher salt
1 pound russet or white potatoes, peeled and cut into ½ inch cubes
3 bay leaves

DIRECTIONS:

First, make the stock. In a large stockpot, combine the water with the vegetable soup powder. Bring the liquid to a boil. Reduce the heat and simmer for 2½ hours.

Prepare the leeks. Trim and discard the dark green tops and tough outer leaves. Cut each leek in half lengthwise, then cut it into thin strips. Put the sliced leeks into a large colander and rinse thoroughly, making sure to remove all dirt. Dry the leeks well.

Heat the oil in a large stockpot until it shimmers. Add the leeks and salt, and reduce the heat to medium. Let the leeks sauté until wilted and very caramelized, about 45 minutes.

Add the broth to the leeks. Add the potatoes and bay leaves and simmer for 2 hours. Remove the bay leaves before serving.

Makes 12 generous servings.

Passover Friendly

Onion Soup

Thanks to some creative vegetarian-friendly methods and lots of caramelized onions, you'll never miss the beef stock in this onion soup.

Pareve

 INGREDIENTS:

1 teaspoon extra-virgin olive oil
5 large white or yellow onions, thinly sliced
2 tablespoons kosher salt
3 tablespoons unsalted margarine
4 cups vegetable stock
2 cups water
4 pinches thyme
3 tablespoons pareve beef soup powder

Corn starch solution:
1 teaspoon corn starch
2 tablespoons water

DIRECTIONS:

Pour 1 teaspoon of the oil into a Dutch oven or large stockpot over high heat. When you see the oil shimmering, reduce the heat to medium and add the onions, salt, and margarine. Sauté the onions, stirring frequently, until they are golden brown and caramelized, 30 to 45 minutes.

Meanwhile, combine the stock, water, thyme, and soup powder in a medium stockpot over high heat. Bring the liquid to a boil. Reduce the heat to low and simmer until the onions finish cooking.

Add the liquid to the pot that contains the onions, reduce the heat to medium-low, and cook for 30 more minutes.

Add the corn starch solution, increase the heat to medium-high, and cook for another 5 to 10 minutes or until the soup thickens.

Serve with crusty bread or crackers.

Makes 12 generous servings.

PASSOVER FRIENDLY TIPS:

If you can't find vegetable stock in a carton, make some using vegetable powder and water. Substitute potato starch for corn starch.

Vegetable Minestrone Soup

Elana's dad, Yaakov Milstein, loves minestrone, so this one's for him. The beans and tomatoes play off each other well, and, like many of the dishes in this book, you won't have to slave in the kitchen all day to eat something special for dinner.

 INGREDIENTS:

4 cups vegetable stock
1 (28-ounce) can crushed tomatoes
1 (28-ounce) can diced tomatoes, drained
2 medium onions, diced
2 red bell peppers, cored and diced
2 tablespoons garlic powder
1 tablespoon dried oregano
2 teaspoons Italian seasoning
4 teaspoons kosher salt
1 (15.5-ounce) can red kidney beans, drained
1 (15.5-ounce) can light kidney beans, drained
1(15.5-ounce) can cannellini beans, drained

DIRECTIONS:

Add all ingredients to a 5- or 6-quart slow cooker and cook on low for 6 to 8 hours.

Makes 12 generous servings.

Slow Cooker Lentil Stew

Let's face it: everything's better in the slow cooker. For this dish, spend a few minutes in the morning opening some cans and packages, and spend the rest of the day looking forward to a stick-to-your-ribs-good dinner.

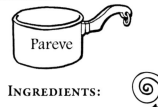

Pareve

 INGREDIENTS:

1 (16-ounce) bag dry lentils, rinsed and dried
6 cups vegetable stock
1 cup water
2 teaspoons salt
2 cloves garlic, minced
2 onions, chopped
2 celery stalks, chopped
2 carrots, chopped
1 (14.5-ounce) can diced tomatoes, including liquid
1 (6-ounce) can tomato paste
2 bay leaves
3 large white button mushrooms (about 2 cups), thinly sliced
1 green onion, chopped

DIRECTIONS:

Add all ingredients, except the green onions, to a slow cooker and cook on high for 6 to 8 hours.

Taste the stew every so often and add salt as needed.

When serving the stew, sprinkle green onions on top for garnish.

Makes 4 to 6 servings.

Mexican Bean Salad with Honey-Lime Dressing

One of our favorite restaurants has a killer honey-lime dressing. We liked it so much,
we created our own version and combined it with this great (and healthy) bean salad.

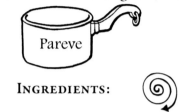

Pareve

INGREDIENTS:

Salad:
1 (11-ounce) can corn, drained
1 (15.5-ounce) can black beans, rinsed and drained
1(15.5-ounce) can light kidney beans, rinsed and drained
4 small plum tomatoes, diced
1 red onion, diced
2 red bell peppers, diced

Dressing:
1 teaspoon ground cumin
2 tablespoons lime juice
½ tablespoon table salt
¼ teaspoon ground black pepper
2 tablespoons safflower or vegetable oil
3 tablespoons honey
½ teaspoon chili powder

 DIRECTIONS:

In a medium saucepan, heat the corn and beans for about 5 minutes.

In a medium bowl, combine all of the dressing ingredients vigorously with a whisk.
Set aside.

Place the beans and corn in a large bowl and add the tomatoes, onion, and bell peppers. Pour the dressing on top.

Let the salad sit for at least 2 hours before serving.

Make 2 to 4 servings.

Greek Pasta Salad

One of our longtime friends, Heidi Cox, gave us this recipe. It's a great way to transform pasta into a Greek treat.

Dairy

 INGREDIENTS:

1 (16-ounce) box penne pasta
1–2 teaspoons extra-virgin olive oil
1 cucumber, peeled and diced
2 medium plum tomatoes, diced
1 red onion, finely diced
4 ounces crumbled feta cheese

Dressing:
½ cup extra-virgin olive oil
4 tablespoons red wine vinegar
Juice of 1 lemon
2 cloves garlic, minced
1 teaspoon salt
1 teaspoon dried oregano

 DIRECTIONS:

Cook pasta according to the package directions in salted water. Drain and rinse well. Place the pasta in a large bowl and coat it with 1 to 2 teaspoons of olive oil.

To the pasta, add the cucumbers, tomatoes, red onion, and feta cheese. Mix together.

In a separate bowl, whisk together all dressing ingredients, then pour the dressing over the salad. Mix together.

Makes 4 servings.

Pasta Salad with Balsamic Dressing

There's no need to drown pasta with mayonnaise for your next potluck outing. The balsamic dressing coats the pasta and vegetables swimmingly. This salad will make you the star anywhere you take it.

Pareve

 INGREDIENTS:

1 (12-ounce) box tricolor rotini
1 red onion, diced
1 red bell pepper, diced
½ bag (about 8 ounces) frozen broccoli, thawed and roughly chopped
1 cup shredded carrots

Dressing:
1 (0.7-ounce) salad dressing packet, Italian style
¼ cup balsamic vinegar
3 tablespoons water
½ cup extra-virgin olive oil

DIRECTIONS:

Cook pasta according to the package directions in salted water. Drain the pasta, rinse well, and place it in a large bowl.

Add the bell pepper, red onion, broccoli, and shredded carrots to the pasta.

Whisk the dressing ingredients together in a separate bowl. Pour the dressing over the pasta mixture.

Refrigerate the salad overnight so the pasta can absorb the dressing.

(You may want to mix another batch of the dressing to pour over the pasta salad before serving.)

Makes 4 servings.

(Mashed) Potato Salad

This salad gets its name from the fact that baking potatoes are very easily mashed. So if you boil the potatoes a bit longer, you'll have delectable cold mashed potatoes. If you want a more traditional potato salad, either cook the potatoes for less time or use red potatoes instead.

 INGREDIENTS:

3 medium baking potatoes, peeled and cubed
2 green onions, cut into small pieces (greens only)
1 tablespoon kosher salt

Dressing:
1 (0.7-ounce) salad dressing packet
¼ cup white vinegar
3 tablespoons water
½ cup extra-virgin olive oil

DIRECTIONS:

Fill a medium saucepan about two-thirds of the way with water. Cover the pan and bring the water to a boil over high heat. Lower the heat to medium, then add the potatoes and the salt.

While the potatoes are cooking, combine the dressing ingredients.

When the potatoes are soft but not mushy (about 10-15 minutes, a.k.a. fork tender), pour them into a colander and drain the water.

Put the potatoes into a bowl. Add the dressing and the green onions. Stir to combine. Refrigerate the potato salad overnight.

Makes 2 to 4 servings.

Israeli Salad

Straight from the Jewish State, here's a chopped salad from Elana's dad. It goes well with pretty much anything.

Pareve

 INGREDIENTS:

1 green bell pepper, finely diced
1 orange bell pepper, finely diced
1 red bell pepper, finely diced
1 large cucumber, finely diced
1 handful fresh parsley, finely diced
3 Roma tomatoes, finely diced
4 radishes, finely diced
2 handfuls shredded carrots
5 leaves romaine lettuce (about ½ head), chopped very small
1 hard-boiled egg, diced (optional)
3 small pickles, diced (optional)
2 green onions, diced (optional)
4 tablespoons extra-virgin olive oil

DIRECTIONS:

Combine all ingredients in a large bowl, adding the oil last. Let the salad sit overnight.

Makes 4 servings.

Passover Friendly

Falafel Salad

You don't need to venture to your local Middle Eastern place any more for this treat. And there's no bean soaking involved!

Pareve

 INGREDIENTS:

1 head romaine lettuce, chopped into bite-sized pieces
1 large cucumber, cut into ½ inch pieces
1 cup shredded carrots
3 Roma tomatoes, chopped into bite-sized pieces
1 red, yellow, or orange bell pepper, diced
4–6 falafel balls, either made from a mix or store-bought
Tahina dressing (see recipe on next page)

 DIRECTIONS:

Combine the vegetables in a large bowl and mix well.

Add the cooked falafel balls. Spoon the tahina dressing on top.

Enjoy with pita bread or your favorite crackers.

Makes 2 servings.

Tahina Dressing

Elana's dad has been making this dressing since his youth in Tel Aviv. It was one of the first things Elana made when she was a kid, and it epitomizes our connection to both Israel and Elana's family.

Pareve

 INGREDIENTS:

1 (17.5-ounce) plastic bottle ready-made seasoned tahina paste
10 ounces water
8 small lemons (enough to make 10 ounces of lemon juice)
5 cloves garlic, finely minced
1 big handful fresh parsley, finely minced
Paprika, to taste
Ground black pepper, to taste

DIRECTIONS:

Pour the bottle of tahina paste into a large mixing bowl.

Juice the lemons (for ease, you can use an electric juicer or a hand lemon squeezer). Pour the lemon juice and water into the empty tahina bottle, and stir. While stirring, scrape down the sides of the bottle to pick up any remaining tahina paste.

Pour the liquid mixture into the bowl with the tahina paste. Add the garlic, parsley, paprika, and ground black pepper.

Combine all ingredients using a hand mixer until very well mixed, 3 to 5 minutes.

For best results, let the dressing marinate overnight so it will thicken.

Makes about 8 servings.

Sides
and
Sandwiches

Sesame Noodles

As a kid, Rob used to love these noodles, especially during the summer. The toasted sesame seeds add a burst of flavor and permeate every bite.

 INGREDIENTS:

¼ cup sesame seeds
2 tablespoons sesame oil
1 tablespoon vegetable oil
½ cup soy sauce
½ cup light rice vinegar
6 cloves garlic, minced
¼ cup white sugar
1 (14.5-ounce) package thin spaghetti
1 bunch (about 8) green onions, chopped small (greens only)
1 cup shredded carrots, chopped

DIRECTIONS:

Preheat a dry, medium-sized saucepan over medium heat for 3 minutes.

Toast the sesame seeds for 5 minutes, stirring occasionally.

Add the sesame oil and warm for 2 minutes, stirring to combine.

Reduce the heat to low. Add the vegetable oil and soy sauce and stir continuously for 2 minutes.

Add the rice vinegar and heat for 3 minutes.

Increase the heat to medium. Add the garlic and heat for 5 to 10 minutes, until the sauce starts to boil.

Add the sugar and stir constantly until it dissolves, 1 to 2 minutes.

Remove the sauce from the heat and set it aside.

Make the spaghetti according to package directions in salted water. Drain the noodles and place them in a large bowl. Pour the sauce over the noodles. Add the green onions and carrots.

Stir until everything is combined. Let the mixture cool, about 1 hour, before putting it in the refrigerator for at least 6 hours (overnight is best).

Makes 4 to 6 servings.

Jasmine Rice Pilaf

Trust us, you won't be buying boxed rice mixes after making this dish. The only hard part will be waiting until it's done to try it.

 INGREDIENTS:

2 teaspoons extra-virgin olive oil
2 medium white or yellow onions, diced
2 teaspoons kosher salt
2 cups vegetable stock
1 cup jasmine rice

DIRECTIONS:

Warm up a small frying pan over high heat. Pour the olive oil into the pan. When you see the oil shimmering, reduce the heat to medium-high and add the onions and the salt. Sauté the onions for about 20 minutes.

While the onions are cooking, prepare the rice in a medium saucepan. Pour the stock into the saucepan and bring it to a boil over high heat. (Covering the pan will make the stock boil more quickly, but you need to keep an eye on it.) When the stock boils, add the rice, reduce the heat to low, and cover the pan.

After the rice has absorbed the stock (20 to 25 minutes), taste the rice to make sure it's soft. If you find that the rice is undercooked, don't panic. Just add about ¼ cup of water and let it absorb. Repeat, if necessary, until the rice is soft.

When the rice is done, take the pan off the heat and add the onions. Stir vigorously to combine. Serve immediately.

Makes 4 servings.

Garlic Mashed Potatoes

We're addicted to spuds, as you probably can tell. This garlicky goodness is the perfect side dish for any meal. Try it with our brisket (p. 115) or meatballs (p. 113).

Pareve

 INGREDIENTS:

1 tablespoon plus 2 teaspoons kosher salt
Ground black pepper, to taste
4 pounds Yukon Gold potatoes, peeled and sliced
4–6 cloves garlic, minced
1 large sweet onion (Spanish or Vidalia), sliced
6 tablespoons unsalted stick margarine
½ cup soy milk
1 tablespoon extra-virgin olive oil
Paprika, to taste

DIRECTIONS:

Preheat the oven to 350 degrees.

Boil the potatoes in water with 1 tablespoon of kosher salt and ground black pepper to taste. Boil until the potatoes are soft but not mushy (a.k.a. fork tender).

Sauté the onions in olive oil with 2 teaspoons kosher salt over medium heat until the onions are soft, 10 to 15 minutes.

When the onions are fully cooked, clear a space in the middle of the pan and add the garlic. Cook until you can smell the garlic, 1 to 2 minutes. Remove from the heat.

Drain the potatoes and put them back into the pan. Mash away.

Add the garlic, onions, and margarine. Stir until everything is incorporated and the potatoes start to soften.

Pour in the soy milk and stir.

Put the mixture into an oven-safe container. Sprinkle paprika on top of the potatoes.

Bake uncovered for about 10 minutes. Do not leave the potatoes in the oven for too long or they will dry out.

Makes 4 servings.

PASSOVER FRIENDLY TIP:

Add another 2 tablespoons of margarine instead of the soy milk. Or, if you don't mind it being dairy, substitute skim milk for soy milk.

Roasted Potatoes and Vegetables

Got company coming over and can't think of a side dish? Just cut up a few things and roast them in the oven for 45 minutes. That's the best part of this dish: minimum effort, maximum result.

 INGREDIENTS:

1 pound medium yellow or red potatoes, quartered or cut smaller (depending on size)
1 red or yellow bell pepper, thinly sliced
2 medium yellow onions, thinly sliced
6–8 garlic cloves, peeled but whole
1 (8–10 ounce package) white or crimini mushrooms, chopped
At least 8 tablespoons extra-virgin olive oil (as needed)
2 tablespoons kosher salt

 DIRECTIONS:

Preheat the oven to 400 degrees.

Place all the vegetables on an extra-large cookie sheet. Coat them generously with olive oil and salt. Stir with your hands so all the vegetables are coated.

Place the cookie sheet in the oven for 30 to 45 minutes. Keep a close eye on the vegetables so that they don't burn.

When everything is cooked, you can either discard the garlic or crush it and serve with the rest of the vegetables. Place all the vegetables in a large bowl or on a platter.

Makes 4 servings.

Passover Friendly

Potato Kugel

This kugel recipe has been part of Rob's family for a while. It's survived the generations and many moves.

 INGREDIENTS:

5 medium russet potatoes, cut in half
4 medium yellow onions, cut in half
3 extra-large eggs
¼ cup matzah meal
Kosher salt, to taste
Ground black pepper, to taste
3 tablespoons vegetable oil

DIRECTIONS:

Preheat the oven to 400 degrees.

One by one, place the potatoes and onions into a food processor, with the shredding blade attached. Shred all the potatoes and onions together.

Squeeze out all excess liquid from the potato mixture by placing small batches into a kitchen towel.

Place the potato mixture into a bowl and add the eggs. Mix thoroughly.

Add the matzah meal and 2 pinches each of salt and ground black pepper. Mix well.

Pour the oil into a 9 × 13 nonstick pan and place it in the oven to heat it up. Take the pan out after 5 to 10 minutes. Add the mixture to the pan in a smooth, even layer.

Cook for about 1 hour, or until the top is brown.

Note: This recipe may also be used to make latkes. Instead of putting the potato mixture into a pan and heating it in the oven, you would heat oil in a pan on the stove, make small, flat disks of the potato mixture, and fry them, browning on both sides.

Makes 6 to 8 servings.

Passover Friendly

Farfel Stuffing

Every year on Passover, Rob's mom, Libby Saypol, makes this dish for one of our seders. It's a great way to please your guests and it's vegetarian, too.

Pareve

INGREDIENTS:

1 tablespoon extra-virgin olive oil
2 medium yellow onions, diced
2–3 stalks celery, finely chopped
2 teaspoons kosher salt
⅓ cup fresh parsley, finely chopped
3 cups farfel
2 cups vegetable stock
½ teaspoon ground black pepper
1 tablespoon onion powder
½ tablespoon paprika

 DIRECTIONS:

Preheat the oven to 400 degrees.

Pour 2 teaspoons of the oil into a 10- or 12-inch high-sided pan over high heat. When you see the oil shimmering, add the onions and 1 teaspoon of salt. Reduce the heat to medium-high and let the onions cook for 5 minutes.

Add the celery along with another teaspoon of salt. Cook for another 10 minutes until the vegetables are very soft and translucent.

In a very large bowl, mix the farfel, onion, celery, and parsley, stirring vigorously to combine. Add the vegetable stock and stir again.

Add the ground black pepper, onion powder, and paprika, stirring again so everything is combined. Let the mixture sit in the bowl for 5 minutes or until all of the liquid has been absorbed.

Brush an 8 × 8 nonstick baking pan with 1 teaspoon of olive oil, using a pastry brush so every surface is nicely coated. Spoon the farfel mixture into the pan.

Bake uncovered for 30 minutes.

Makes 4 servings.

Passover Friendly

Corn Bread

There's no better accompaniment to chili (see p. 55) than this treat. It's got a crispy crust and a soft middle. Enjoy it by itself or with some butter or margarine.

INGREDIENTS:

2 cups unbleached all-purpose flour
1 cup cornmeal
4 teaspoons baking powder
¾ teaspoon table salt
¼ cup vegetable oil
1 cup sugar
3 extra-large eggs, beaten
1 cup milk (skim or soy)

 ## DIRECTIONS:

Preheat the oven to 400 degrees.

In a bowl, combine the flour, cornmeal, baking powder, and salt. Set aside.

In another bowl, combine the oil and sugar, mixing well. Add the beaten eggs.

To the oil mixture, add half the milk and mix well. Add half the flour mixture and mix again. Repeat with the remaining milk and flour.

Mix the batter thoroughly and pour it into a greased 9x13 nonstick pan.

Bake uncovered for 20 to 25 minutes or until a toothpick comes out clean.

Makes 4 to 6 servings.

Portabella Mushroom Sandwiches

Elana's sister, Gershona Fein, shared this recipe with us on a trip east a while back.

INGREDIENTS:

1 package portabella mushroom caps or crimini mushrooms, sliced very thin
¼ cup balsamic vinegar
½ cup extra-virgin olive oil
½ cup Parmesan cheese, shredded
2 pita loaves

 DIRECTIONS:

Preheat oven to 350 degrees.

Mix the vinegar and olive oil in an airtight container.

Add the mushrooms to the container. Place the lid on the container and shake to coat the mushrooms evenly. Marinate the mushrooms in the oil and vinegar overnight (or for an hour, if you are short on time).

Pour the mushrooms, oil, and vinegar into a 10- or 12-inch high-sided pan over medium-high heat.

When the liquid starts to boil and the mushrooms are soft (about 10 minutes), remove the pan from the heat.

Slice each pita in half.

Place equal amounts of the mushroom mixture into each pita pocket.

Place an equal amount of Parmesan cheese in each pita. Place the pita pockets on a cookie sheet.

Heat uncovered in the oven until the cheese is melted, 8 to 10 minutes.

Makes 2 servings.

Tuna Melts with Caramelized Onion

So many people love tuna melts. Our version boasts a layer of caramelized onions. The onions add a special touch that goes swimmingly with the saltiness of the Parmesan cheese.

Dairy

INGREDIENTS:

4 tablespoons extra-virgin olive oil
1 medium yellow onion, diced
3 teaspoons kosher salt, preferably freshly ground
2 hamburger buns (or anything similar), split into 4 halves
Freshly shredded Parmesan cheese, to taste

Tuna salad:
1 (6-ounce) can tuna fish
2 tablespoons mayonnaise
1 stalk celery, finely chopped (optional)

 ## DIRECTIONS:

Prepare the tuna salad and set aside.

Preheat the oven to 350 degrees.

Pour 3 tablespoons of the oil into a 10- or 12-inch high-sided pan over high heat. When you see the oil shimmering, add the onions and 2 teaspoons of salt, and sauté for about 5 minutes.

Reduce the heat to medium. Sauté the onions for 10 to 15 additional minutes, until the onions are soft and slightly brown. Place the onions in a separate bowl.

Pour the remaining tablespoon of olive oil into the same pan, then add the bread. Let each side of the bread brown for about 5 minutes until it is slightly brown but not burned.

Place the 4 halves of bread onto a large cookie sheet. Then put down a layer of onions on each piece of bread, dividing the onions equally among the 4 halves. Do the same thing with the tuna salad.

Sprinkle as much cheese on top as you'd like.

Bake uncovered until the cheese is nicely melted, 5 to 10 minutes.

Makes 2 to 4 servings.

Vegetarian Sloppy Joe Sandwiches

One of our friends, Stacy Rabkin, first turned us on to these meat-free sandwiches. Not only do the vegetables add a great touch, but it's sure to fool your carnivorous friends.

Pareve

INGREDIENTS:

1 tablespoon extra-virgin olive oil
2 medium yellow onions, thinly sliced
2 teaspoons kosher salt
1 medium yellow, red, or orange bell pepper, chopped
12 ounces vegetarian ground meat
1 (15.5-ounce) can of sloppy joe sauce
1 (6-ounce) can tomato paste
Bread or flour tortillas

 ## DIRECTIONS:

Pour the oil into a 10- or 12-inch high-sided pan over high heat. When you see the oil shimmering, add the onions and 2 teaspoons of salt, and reduce the heat to medium. Sauté for about 5 minutes.

Add the bell pepper and sauté for another 5 minutes until all pieces are soft and slightly brown.

Add the vegetarian ground meat and sauté until the protein is cooked, 5 to 7 minutes more.

Add the sloppy joe sauce and tomato paste and cook for about 5 minutes, stirring frequently. It might bubble, but that's OK. You can always lower the heat.

Serve immediately with your favorite bread or flour tortillas.

Makes 4 to 6 servings.

Easy Vegetable Sandwich

This is the fastest recipe in the book. Enough said.

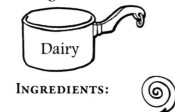

 INGREDIENTS:

1 tablespoon ranch dressing (or other dressing)
1–2 slices fresh mozzarella cheese
1 small Roma tomato, sliced
1 small roasted red pepper (from a jar)
1 teaspoon liquid from the roasted red pepper jar
1 club roll or similar bread, sliced in half

DIRECTIONS:

Put the dressing on the bread and add the cheese, tomato, and pepper.

Sprinkle the oil from the roasted red pepper jar on the sandwich.

Enjoy with chips or potato salad (see p. 30).

Makes 1 sandwich.

Vegetarian
Main
Dishes

Elana's Famous Vegetarian Chili

Until Rob had this dish, he swore he didn't like chili. But thanks to the slow cooker and just the right amount of spice, this too-good-to-be-vegetarian dish changed his mind forever.

Pareve

 INGREDIENTS:

1 tablespoon olive oil
24 ounces vegetarian ground meat
1 (15.5-ounce) can pinto beans, drained
1 (15.5-ounce) can light kidney beans, drained
1 (15.5-ounce) can dark kidney beans, drained
1 (28-ounce) can stewed tomatoes, with juice
1 (6-ounce) can tomato paste
1 red bell pepper, diced (optional)
1 white or yellow onion, diced (optional)
Chili powder, to taste

DIRECTIONS:

Pour the oil into a 10- or 12-inch high-sided pan over high heat. When you see the oil shimmering, add the vegetarian ground meat and reduce the heat to medium. Sauté for 5 to 7 minutes. (If using bell pepper and onion, you can either sauté them with the meat now, or add them to the slow cooker later with the tomato paste and chili powder.)

Transfer the meat to a 6-quart slow cooker. Add the beans. Pour in the can of stewed tomatoes (juice and all). Fill the stewed tomato can with water and pour that in, too.

Add the tomato paste and chili powder. Stir well.

Cook on low for 8 hours.

Makes 4 to 8 servings.

Vegetarian Hamburger Stew

Elana's mom, Charna Milstein, turned us on to this dish, another slow-cooker wonder.

Pareve

 INGREDIENTS:

1 tablespoon olive oil
24 ounces vegetarian ground meat
2 (15-ounce) cans sliced potatoes, drained
1 (15-ounce) can diced carrots, drained
1 (15-ounce) can sliced French green beans, drained
1 (6-ounce) can tomato paste
1 (48-ounce) bottle low sodium tomato vegetable juice cocktail)

DIRECTIONS:

Pour the oil into a 10- or 12-inch high-sided pan over high heat. When you see the oil shimmering, add the vegetarian ground meat and reduce the heat to medium. Sauté for 5 to 7 minutes.

Transfer the vegetarian meat to a 6-quart slow cooker. Add the potatoes, carrots, and green beans. Add the tomato paste, and pour in the tomato vegetable juice cocktail. Stir well.

Cook on low for 8 hours.

Makes 4 to 6 servings.

Tortilla Española

While we were in Spain, there were only two things we ate more than once: falafel and this treat. It's our take on the traditional potato omelet, which is usually enjoyed for lunch or dinner.

INGREDIENTS:

2 large leeks, prepared as described below
4 tablespoons vegetable oil
2 tablespoons kosher salt
1 pound russet or white potatoes, diced
2 generous tablespoons unsalted butter or margarine
15 ounces egg substitute
¼ cup milk (soy or skim)

 DIRECTIONS:

Prepare the leeks: Trim and discard the dark green tops and tough outer leaves. Cut the leek in half lengthwise, then cut it into thin strips. Put the sliced leeks into a large colander and rinse thoroughly, making sure to remove all dirt. Dry the leeks well.

Pour 1 teaspoon of the oil into a 10- or 12-inch high-sided pan over high heat. When you see the oil shimmering, add the leeks and 1 tablespoon of salt and sauté for 5 to 7 minutes.

Reduce the heat to medium. Add the potatoes, the remaining salt, and the margarine or butter. Sauté for 20 to 25 minutes, until the potatoes are soft and golden brown and the leeks are caramelized.

Add the egg substitute and milk or soy milk. Cover and cook for 5 to 7 minutes (look for the bottom of the eggs to firm up with liquid on top).

Uncover the pan. Use a spatula to cut the eggs into 4 or 6 sections, like you would cut a pie or pizza. Flip each section individually, allowing the uncooked egg to sink to the bottom of the pan.

Cook uncovered for an additional 3 to 5 minutes. Flip again to make sure both sides of the eggs are cooked and slightly brown.

Makes 2 to 4 servings.

PASSOVER FRIENDLY TIP:

Use skim milk.

Fajita Burrito

When we visited Elana's sister in California, she introduced us to vegetarian burritos. Now we make them all the time using this simple and delicious recipe.

INGREDIENTS:

2 teaspoons vegetable oil
1 large yellow onion, diced
1–2 teaspoons kosher salt
1 medium red bell pepper, diced
2 large white button mushrooms, finely chopped
4 ounces Colby-Jack cheese, shredded
1 (15.4-ounce) can refried black beans
Flour tortillas, as needed

DIRECTIONS:

Pour the oil into a 10- or 12-inch high-sided pan over high heat. When you see the oil shimmering, add the onions and the salt. Reduce the heat to medium-high and sauté for 5 minutes. Add the bell pepper and sauté for 5 more minutes.

Add the mushrooms and sauté for 7 to 10 minutes, until all vegetables are very soft.

To assemble the burrito: spread about ⅛ cup of refried black beans down the middle of a tortilla, add cooked vegetables on top of the beans, then cover lightly with the shredded cheese.

Roll up each tortilla and place it seam side down on a microwave-safe plate. Microwave for 30 seconds to melt the cheese and heat the burrito through.

Makes 2 to 4 servings.

Pasta with Homemade Tomato Sauce

Commercials try to convince you that buying bottled tomato sauce with vegetables added is better. However, we think that making the sauce yourself turns a normal pasta dinner into an Italian treat.

Dairy

 INGREDIENTS:

1 (14.5-ounce) package rotini (or any pasta you like)
2 tablespoons extra-virgin olive oil
3 medium yellow onions, diced
1 tablespoon kosher salt
1 (10-ounce) package crimini mushrooms
2 red, yellow, or orange bell peppers, sliced
1 (28-ounce) can tomato sauce
½ cup Parmesan cheese, shredded

DIRECTIONS:

Cook the pasta according to the package directions in salted water. Drain and set aside. (This can be done while the vegetables are cooking, as instructed below.)

Pour the oil into a 10- or 12-inch high-sided pan over high heat. When you see the oil shimmering, add the onions and the salt and sauté for 5 minutes. Reduce the heat to medium.

Add the mushrooms and bell peppers and cook for 15 minutes. Add the tomato sauce and cook for about 10 minutes, stirring frequently, until the flavors combine.

Add the cooked pasta and stir for about 2 minutes, until everything is incorporated.

Sprinkle the cheese on top and serve immediately.

Makes 4 to 6 servings.

Spinach-Mushroom Lasagna

These two vegetables love each other, so why not play Cupid?

 INGREDIENTS:

1 (16-ounce) package lasagna noodles
2 tablespoons extra-virgin olive oil
1 (6-ounce) package sliced portabella mushrooms, quartered
1 teaspoon kosher salt
1 (10-ounce) package frozen chopped spinach, thawed and drained
6 cloves garlic, minced
Dried oregano, to taste
2 cups mozzarella cheese, shredded
¼ cup Parmesan cheese, shredded
1 (28-ounce) can tomato sauce

 DIRECTIONS:

Preheat the oven to 400 degrees.

Cook the pasta according to the package directions in salted water. Drain and set aside.

Pour the oil into a 10- or 12-inch high-sided pan over high heat. When you see the oil shimmering, add the mushrooms and salt. Reduce the heat to medium-high and cook for 5 minutes.

Add the spinach. Sauté for 3 to 5 minutes.

Make a space in the middle of the pan and add the garlic. Sauté until fragrant, about 1 minute.

To assemble the lasagna: Spread a thin layer of sauce on the bottom of a 9 × 13 nonstick baking pan. Place 3 or 4 noodles on top of the sauce layer, followed by enough sauce to cover the noodles. Sprinkle oregano over the sauce, lay down some of the vegetables, and sprinkle on some of the mozzarella cheese. Add the remaining ingredients in the following order: noodles, sauce, oregano, vegetables, mozzarella, noodles, sauce, oregano, vegetables, mozzarella. When all the vegetables have been used, add more sauce, then top with Parmesan cheese.

Bake uncovered until brown and bubbly, about 30 minutes.

Makes 6 to 8 servings.

Roasted Vegetable Lasagna

Roasting the vegetables brings out their sweetness and makes plain tomato sauce taste like it was flown in from Rome. Don't be scared about using real lasagna noodles. They soak up the sauce and make some extra boiling worth the effort.

 INGREDIENTS:

2–3 red bell peppers, thinly sliced
4 medium yellow onions, thinly sliced
6–8 cloves garlic, peeled but whole
1 (10-ounce) package white or crimini mushrooms, chopped
Extra-virgin olive oil as needed (at least 8 tablespoons)
Dried oregano, to taste
1 (16-ounce) package lasagna noodles
1 (28-ounce) can crushed tomatoes
1 (15-ounce) can tomato sauce
3 tablespoons sugar
Kosher salt, to taste
8 ounces mozzarella cheese, shredded
4 ounces Parmesan cheese, shredded

 DIRECTIONS:

Preheat the oven to 400 degrees.

Place the bell peppers, onions, garlic, and mushrooms on an extra-large cookie sheet and coat them generously with olive oil and salt. Stir with your hands so all the vegetables are coated with oil. Sprinkle the vegetables with oregano to taste.

Place the cookie sheet in the oven for 30 to 45 minutes. Keep a close eye on the vegetables so they don't burn.

While the vegetables are roasting, place the crushed tomatoes, tomato sauce, sugar, salt, and oregano in a large saucepan. Cover and simmer over low heat.

Boil the lasagna noodles according to the package directions in salted water.

When the vegetables are done, crush the roasted garlic cloves with a fork to break them up. Then, add the vegetables to the pan with the sauce. Simmer for 10 minutes to let the flavors combine.

To assemble the lasagna: Spread a thin layer of sauce on the bottom of a large nonstick or disposable 9 × 13 baking pan. Place 3 or 4 noodles on top of the sauce layer, then add more sauce on top of the noodles, followed by some of each type of cheese. Add the remaining ingredients in the same order: noodles, sauce, cheese. When all the noodles have been used, add some sauce and cheese on top.

Bake uncovered until brown and bubbly, 20 to 30 minutes.

Makes 6 to 8 servings.

Matzah Lasagna

Passover can be a danger zone for vegetarians, as this holiday is traditionally meat focused. Matzah has never tasted so Italian with this vegetarian main dish.

 INGREDIENTS:

2 tablespoons extra-virgin olive oil
3 teaspoons kosher salt
3 medium yellow onions, diced
1 (10-ounce) package crimini mushrooms
2 red, yellow, or orange bell peppers
1 (28-ounce) can tomato sauce
1 box matzah
8 ounces mozzarella cheese, shredded
4 ounces Parmesan cheese, shredded

 DIRECTIONS:

Preheat the oven to 400 degrees.

Pour 1 tablespoon of the oil into a 10- or 12-inch high-sided pan over high heat. When you see the oil shimmering, add the onions and reduce the heat to medium. Add 2 teaspoons of salt. Cook the onions for about 5 minutes, until they start to soften.

Add the mushrooms and bell peppers along with the last teaspoon of salt. Cook for 15 minutes.

Add the tomato sauce and cook for about 10 minutes, stirring frequently, until the flavors combine.

To assemble the lasagna: Spread a thin layer of sauce on the bottom of a large nonstick or disposable 9 × 13 lasagna pan. Place 3 or 4 pieces of matzah (you might have to break them to fit) on top of the sauce layer. Add more sauce on top of the matzah, followed by some of each type of cheese. Add the remaining ingredients in the same order: matzah, sauce, cheese. When there are three or four layers or you're running out of room in the pan, add one final layer of sauce and Parmesan cheese on top.

Bake uncovered until brown and bubbly, 20 to 30 minutes.

Makes 6 to 8 servings.

Passover Friendly

Sloppy Pasta

Here is another way to enjoy sloppy joes. Be warned: the dish does live up to its name, so be prepared to do laundry shortly after eating.

 INGREDIENTS:

1 (12-ounce) package yolk-free egg noodles (or any pasta you like)
2 tablespoons extra-virgin olive oil
2 medium yellow onions, sliced
1 tablespoon kosher salt
12 ounces vegetarian ground meat
1 (15.5-ounce) can sloppy joe sauce
1 (10.5-ounce) can tomato sauce
1 tablespoon garlic powder (or more if you prefer)
½ cup Parmesan cheese, shredded

 DIRECTIONS:

Cook the pasta according to the package directions in salted water. Drain and set aside. (This can be done while the onions are caramelizing, as instructed below.)

Pour 1 tablespoon of the oil into a 10- or 12-inch high-sided pan over high heat. When you see the oil shimmering, add the onions and reduce the heat to medium. Add the salt and let the onions caramelize until they are golden brown and very soft, about 20 minutes.

Add the vegetarian ground meat and garlic powder and sauté until the meat is cooked, 5 to 7 minutes.

Add the sloppy joe sauce and tomato sauce. Cook for about 10 minutes, stirring frequently. It might bubble, but that's OK. You can always lower the heat.

Add the cooked egg noodles and stir for about 2 minutes, until everything is incorporated.

Serve immediately.

Makes 4 servings.

Mini Pizzas

Want to make pizza at home but don't want to fiddle with the dough? Here's an easy way to get the best of both worlds in a short amount of time without the fuss.

Dairy

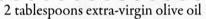

INGREDIENTS:

2 tablespoons extra-virgin olive oil
1 medium yellow onion, diced
2 tablespoons kosher salt
1 (10-ounce) package crimini mushrooms, sliced
1 red, yellow, or orange bell pepper, sliced
1 (14.5-ounce) can tomato sauce
4 low-fat rolls or pita bread (or any similar bread), each split in half
½ cup Parmesan cheese, shredded

 DIRECTIONS:

Preheat the oven to 400 degrees.

Warm up a medium saucepan over high heat and pour the olive oil into the pan. When you see the oil shimmering, add the onions and 1 teaspoon of salt and reduce the heat to medium.

Cook for about 5 minutes, until the onions start to soften. Add the mushrooms and bell peppers and cook for 15 minutes. Add the tomato sauce and cook for about 10 minutes, stirring frequently, until the flavors combine.

Place the bread halves on a large cookie sheet so that they do not overlap. Then, spoon sauce on each piece of bread, dividing the sauce evenly among the 8 halves. Do the same thing with the cheese. Bake until the cheese is nicely melted, 5 to 10 minutes.

Makes 2 to 4 servings.

Vegetarian Paella Risotto

A vegetarian restaurant in Madrid gave us our first taste of this Spanish specialty, which we fell in love with almost as fast as we did with the city itself. The creamy texture and saffron undertones will leave you saying "Me encanta España (I love Spain)."

Pareve

INGREDIENTS:

4 cups vegetable stock
3 tablespoons extra-virgin olive oil
3 yellow onions, thinly sliced
1 tablespoon kosher salt
2 yellow, red, or orange bell peppers, thinly sliced
1 (10-ounce) package crimini mushrooms, sliced
3 garlic cloves, minced
2 (14.5-ounce) cans diced tomatoes
2 cups arborio rice, uncooked
½ tablespoon paprika
½ teaspoon (about 10 strands) saffron
Ground black pepper, to taste

 ## DIRECTIONS:

Pour the vegetable stock into a medium stockpot, add the saffron and bring it to a boil. Reduce the heat to low and simmer throughout the rest of the cooking process.

Meanwhile, pour 1 tablespoon of the oil into a 10- or 12-inch high-sided pan over high heat. When you see the oil shimmering, put in the onions and 1 tablespoon of salt and reduce the heat to medium. Sauté the onions for about 5 minutes.

Add the bell peppers and mushrooms and cook until they are very soft and nearly caramelized, 15 to 20 minutes.

Add the garlic and stir everything for about 1 minute, until you can smell the garlic.

Pour in the tomatoes and stir for 2 minutes. Add the uncooked rice and stir until the liquid from the tomatoes is absorbed, about 3 minutes.

Add the paprika and reduce the heat to medium-low. Next, add 2 ladles of the vegetable stock and cook until the stock is absorbed. Repeat this process until you've used all of the stock, about 1 hour.

At that point, the rice should be perfectly cooked. If you find that the rice is undercooked, don't panic. Just add about ¼ cup of water and let it absorb. Repeat, if necessary, until the rice is soft.

Makes 4 to 6 servings.

Citrus Stir-Fried Rice and Vegetables

The first time Rob invited Elana over for dinner, he made Martin Yan's tri-flavored chicken to wow her. (As you can tell, it worked.) This is an evolution of that dish, keeping intact the citrus trio of lemon, lime, and orange juice.

Pareve

INGREDIENTS:

1 cup jasmine rice
1 (14-ounce) package extra-firm tofu, drained and cut into approximately ½-inch pieces
4 tablespoons vegetable oil
2 medium yellow or white onions, sliced into bite-size pieces
1 medium red, yellow, or orange bell pepper, sliced into small pieces
1 (8-ounce) package white button mushrooms, sliced into small pieces

Sauce:
Juice of 1 small lime
¼ cup orange juice (from a carton or bottle)
¼ cup lemon juice (fresh or bottled)
½ cup low-sodium soy sauce
⅛ cup honey

Corn starch solution:
1 teaspoon corn starch
⅓ cup water

 DIRECTIONS:

Prepare the rice according to the package directions. This usually takes 20 to 30 minutes. If you do this first, the rice will be ready by the time you need it at the end of the recipe. (Don't forget the rice while you're doing everything else.)

Pour 2 tablespoons of the oil into a 10- or 12-inch high-sided pan over high heat. When you see the oil shimmering, add the tofu and reduce the heat to medium. The tofu will brown in 10 to 15 minutes if you turn it every once in a while.

While the tofu is browning, pour 1 teaspoon of the oil into another 10- or 12-inch high-sided pan over high heat. When you see the oil shimmering, add the onions and reduce the heat to medium. Sauté the onions for about 5 minutes. Add the bell pepper and mushrooms and sauté for about 15 minutes.

Assemble the sauce in a separate bowl. Into a third bowl, mix the corn starch solution.

Add the tofu to the pan that contains the onions, peppers, and mushrooms. Stir to combine for 3 to 5 minutes. Add the rice and sauté for a minute to combine. Add the sauce and combine for 3 minutes.

Stir the corn starch solution for about 30 seconds, until all the starch is dissolved. Pour the corn starch solution into the pan. Increase the heat to medium-high and stir until the sauce bubbles and thickens, 3 to 5 minutes.

The finished product should look like paella or risotto.

Makes 2 to 4 servings.

Garlic Noodles

We've had these kinds of noodles in a few Chinese restaurants and always enjoyed them. The garlic taste is present but not overpowering. It's a nice Asian dish to enjoy by itself or as part of a larger meal.

Ingredients:

½ box (about 7 ounces) thin spaghetti
2 heads of garlic, cloves separated, skins removed
½ cup plus 1 teaspoon vegetable oil
1 teaspoon kosher salt
2 green onions, chopped small
¼ cup shredded carrots, chopped
3 large garlic cloves, minced

 ## Directions:

Boil the pasta according to the package directions in salted water. Drain and set aside.

Pour the ½ cup of vegetable oil into a 10- or 12-inch high-sided pan over high heat. When you see the oil shimmering, reduce the heat to medium-low.

Add the 2 heads of garlic. Cook for 15 minutes, stirring occasionally, until the garlic is nearly burnt. Remove the garlic from the pan and discard.

To the garlic-infused oil, add the green onions and carrots and sauté for 5 to 10 minutes until both are soft. Add the minced garlic and cook for 2 minutes.

Add the cooked pasta and remaining teaspoon of oil (which will be helpful in keeping the pasta loose) and sauté for 5 minutes. The pasta will get a little brown but not burnt.

Makes 4 servings.

Crustless Quiche

The inspiration for this dish comes from Elana's Aunt Ethel, a very talented cook. We've lightened up her version a bit. Really any vegetables can be used for this dish.

Dairy

 INGREDIENTS:

2 tablespoons extra-virgin olive oil
3 medium yellow or white onions, finely chopped
4 teaspoons kosher salt
1 bunch asparagus, chopped into ½-inch pieces
4 tablespoons unsalted margarine
1 (15-ounce) container egg substitute or 7 jumbo eggs, beaten
1 cup flour
1 cup milk (soy or skim)
1 teaspoon baking powder
1 (8-ounce) block 75% reduced-fat sharp cheddar cheese, shredded

 DIRECTIONS:

Preheat the oven to 350 degrees.

Pour the oil into a 10- or 12-inch high-sided pan over medium-high heat. Add the onions and 2 teaspoons of kosher salt. Sauté for 5 minutes.

Add the asparagus along with another teaspoon of salt. Reduce the heat to medium and sauté for 15 minutes, until the asparagus is soft.

Place the margarine in a 9 × 13 nonstick baking pan. Put the pan in the oven until the margarine is melted, 3 to 5 minutes. Remove and set aside.

While the margarine is melting in the oven, place the egg substitute, flour, milk, baking powder, and remaining teaspoon of salt into a large bowl. Mix well. Add the cheese and vegetables to the bowl. Mix well again.

Spoon everything into the baking pan and bake for 35 minutes.

Cool slightly (5 to 10 minutes) before serving.

Makes 6 to 8 servings.

PASSOVER FRIENDLY TIP:

Use Matzah cake meal instead of flour.

Low Fat Mac and Cheese

We often joke that "low fat" usually means "low taste." Well, not for this dish. You'll never miss a thing in our take on an American classic.

 INGREDIENTS:

½ box elbow macaroni (makes about 4 cups of cooked macaroni)
2 cups milk (skim or soy)
2 tablespoons margarine
1 medium or large white or yellow onion, minced
½ teaspoon salt
1 tablespoon corn starch
1 (8-ounce) block 75% reduced-fat sharp cheddar cheese, shredded

DIRECTIONS:

Cook the macaroni according to the package directions in salted water. Drain and set aside.

Reserve 2 tablespoons of the milk from the 2 cups and set it aside.

In a large saucepan or Dutch oven, heat the margarine. Add the onions and the salt. Cook the onions until they are soft and translucent, 10 to 15 minutes.

In a separate bowl, make a corn starch solution. Whisk together the corn starch and the reserved 2 tablespoons of milk.

When the onions are soft, add the remaining milk, and bring to a boil. Add the corn starch solution. Combine until the mixture becomes thicker, 3 to 5 minutes. Reduce the heat to low and add the cheese. When the cheese has melted, add the macaroni and mix well.

Remove from heat, cover, and let rest for 3 to 5 minutes.

Makes 4 to 6 servings.

Eggplant Schnitzel Cacciatore

While blending two recipes and two cultures, we've created a dish that is worth the extra effort. After eating this, you'll never have plain spaghetti again—unless of course you make your own sauce (like we do on p. 60).

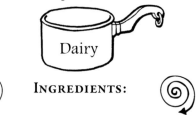

Dairy

INGREDIENTS:

1 (14.5-ounce) package thin spaghetti
1 medium or large firm eggplant, peeled, dehydrated, and sliced (as described below)
5–6 tablespoons kosher salt
1–2 cups all-purpose unbleached flour (use as needed)
2 teaspoons garlic powder
2 teaspoons onion powder
2 extra-large eggs, beaten
1 package (2 cups) Panko bread crumbs (use as needed)
1½ cups plus 2 tablespoons extra-virgin olive oil
3 medium white or yellow onions, diced
1 (10-ounce) package crimini mushrooms, thinly sliced
3 cloves garlic, minced
2 (14.5-ounce) cans Italian-style stewed tomatoes
Shredded Parmesan cheese, to taste

 DIRECTIONS:

Cook the spaghetti in salted water according to the package directions.

Peel the eggplant, cut off the ends, and slice it into ½-inch circular disks. Place the eggplant in a large colander, in layers, with about 1 tablespoon of salt on each layer. Insert a paper towel between the layers to absorb any excess liquid. When you have finished layering the eggplant, place a stockpot (full of water and heavy) on top. Let the eggplant stand for 60 to 90 minutes until it is a little brown and dehydrated.

Set up a breading assembly line: one bowl with the flour, garlic powder, and onion powder; one bowl with the beaten eggs; and one bowl with the bread crumbs.

To bread the eggplant, dip a piece of eggplant into the flour mixture and shake off any excess. Dip the eggplant into the egg, coating the entire piece, and then into the bread crumbs, making sure the piece is fully covered. Set each piece aside on a plate as you bread the rest.

To fry the eggplant, heat 1½ cups of olive oil in a 10- or 12-inch high-sided saucepan. When you see the oil shimmering, put in 3 or 4 pieces of eggplant and fry on each side for about 6 minutes until they're golden brown.

Let the eggplant cool on a paper-towel-lined plate while the others are frying. You also can put the eggplant pieces (after they've drained on the paper towels) onto a baking sheet and then into a 200-degree oven to keep warm.

Meanwhile, pour 2 tablespoons of oil into another 10- or 12-inch high-sided pan over high heat. When you see the oil shimmering, add the onions and 2 tablespoons of kosher salt, and sauté for 5 to 10 minutes until the onions soften. Add the mushrooms, reduce the heat to medium, and sauté for 10 to 15 more minutes, until the mixture is soft and brown. Add the minced garlic and cook for 1 minute. Add the tomatoes and sauté for about 10 minutes, crushing the tomatoes as they cook.

Add the cooked spaghetti to the pan and mix well. Cook for 10 to 15 minutes, until everything is piping hot.

Serve the eggplant on a plate, covered with the pasta. Sprinkle Parmesan cheese on top as desired.

Makes 4 to 6 servings.

Eggplant Parmesan Casserole

If you smile just the right way, Elana will admit she really only likes eggplant in this form. So we ask that you make this for the eggplant doubters in your crowd—and then let us know how many people you converted.

Dairy

INGREDIENTS:

1 large firm eggplant or 2 medium ones, peeled, dehydrated, and sliced (as described below)
5–6 tablespoons kosher salt
1–2 cups all-purpose unbleached flour (use as needed)
2 teaspoons garlic powder
2 teaspoons onion powder
2 extra-large eggs, beaten
1 package (2 cups) Panko bread crumbs (use as needed)
5 tablespoons extra-virgin olive oil
4 medium yellow onions, diced
1 (10-ounce) package crimini mushrooms, thinly sliced
3 cloves garlic
1 (28-ounce) can crushed tomatoes
8 ounces Parmesan cheese, shredded

 DIRECTIONS:

Preheat the oven to 400 degrees.

Peel the eggplant, cut off the ends, and slice it into ½-inch circular disks. Place the eggplant in a large colander, in layers, with about 1 tablespoon of salt on each layer. Insert a paper towel between the layers to absorb any excess liquid. When you have finished layering the eggplant, place a stockpot (full of water and heavy) on top. Let the eggplant stand for 60 to 90 minutes until it is a little brown and dehydrated.

Set up a breading assembly line: one bowl with the flour, garlic powder, and onion powder; one bowl with the beaten eggs; and one bowl with the bread crumbs.

To bread the eggplant, dip a piece of eggplant into the flour mixture and shake off any excess. Dip the eggplant into the egg, coating the entire piece, and then into the bread crumbs, making sure the piece is fully covered. Set each piece aside on a plate as you bread the rest.

Pour about 3 tablespoons of olive oil onto a large cookie sheet and spread evenly. Place the eggplant on the cookie sheet, making sure that none of the pieces overlap. (Use two cookie sheets if needed.) Bake for 10 to 15 minutes per side, until the eggplant is golden brown.

Pour 2 tablespoons of oil into 10- or 12-inch high-sided pan over medium heat. When the oil shimmers, add the onions and 1 tablespoon of salt and sauté for 5 minutes. Add the mushrooms and sauté until very soft, 5 to 10 minutes. Add the minced garlic and sauté 1 minute. Add the tomatoes, reduce the heat to medium-low, and warm through for about 10 minutes. (You can keep it on low heat for up to 20 minutes.)

When the eggplant and sauce are done, it's time for the assembly. Spread a thin layer of sauce on the bottom of a 9 × 13 nonstick baking pan. Place the eggplant pieces on top, leaving very little space between the pieces. Spread another layer of sauce on top of the eggplant, then sprinkle on some of the Parmesan cheese. Repeat, creating layers, until all of the ingredients have been used. The top layer should be Parmesan cheese.

Bake for 20 to 30 minutes, until the cheese is melted and flavors are combined.

Makes 6 to 8 servings.

Mexican Shepherd's Pie

We're not sure if there are any shepherds in Mexico, but we think you'll like this dish anyway. It takes our awesome corn bread and puts it on top of some beans, vegetables and cheese. If you'd like a thinner corn bread layer, you always can halve that part of the recipe.

Dairy

INGREDIENTS:

3 tablespoons vegetable oil
2 teaspoons kosher salt
2 onions, chopped
1 red pepper, chopped
2 cloves garlic, minced
1 (14 ounce) can diced tomatoes, with liquid
Pinch cumin
Pinch chili powder
⅔ cup vegetable juice
1 (15.5 ounce) can black beans, drained and rinsed
1 (15.5 ounce) can pinto beans, drained and rinsed
1 (8 ounce) block 75% reduced fat cheddar cheese

Corn bread batter:
2 cups unbleached all purpose flour
1 cup corn meal
4 teaspoons baking powder
¾ teaspoon table salt
¼ cup vegetable oil
1 cup sugar
3 extra large eggs
1 cup milk (skim or soy)

Preheat oven to 350.

Pour the oil into a 10- or 12-inch high-sided pan and set on high heat. When you see the oil shimmering, put in the onions and kosher salt and reduce the heat to medium. Sauté the onions for 5-10 minutes until they start to soften.

Add the red peppers and cook for about 5 minutes.

Add the garlic and sauté for 1 minute.

Add the beans and diced tomatoes and sauté for 5 minutes. Add the spices and sauté for 1 minute more. Add the vegetable juice and sauté for another 1-2 minutes.

Put the vegetables and beans on the bottom of a 9x13 non stick pan. Sprinkle the cheese on top of that mixture.

Next, create the corn bread batter: combine flour, corn meal, baking powder, and salt in a bowl.

In another bowl, combine the oil and sugar well. Add the beaten eggs to the oil and sugar. To this mixture, add half the milk and mix well. Add half the flour mixture and mix again. Repeat with the rest of the milk and flour. Mix entire batter thoroughly.

Pour the batter on top of the beans, vegetables, and cheese.

Bake for 40-45 minutes until a toothpick comes out clean from the corn bread.

Moses Pie

This is our interpretation of the British classic. (Moses was a shepherd; get it?)

 INGREDIENTS:

4 medium baking potatoes, peeled and thinly sliced (using a mandolin, for example)
½ cup extra-virgin olive oil
½ cup kosher salt, divided
½ teaspoon ground black pepper
1 large yellow onion, diced
24 ounces vegetarian ground meat
1 tablespoon ground cumin
1 tablespoon garlic powder
2 (15.5-ounce) cans corn (no salt added), drained

DIRECTIONS:

Preheat the oven to 400 degrees.

Spread about 5 tablespoons of olive oil onto a very large cookie sheet, coating evenly. Place the sliced potatoes on the sheet so that they do not overlap. Sprinkle about 2 tablespoons of salt and the ground black pepper over the potatoes.

Bake for 30 to 40 minutes, flipping the potatoes halfway through and adding another 2 tablespoons of salt when you flip them.

Meanwhile, pour 1 tablespoon of oil into a 10- or 12-inch high-sided pan over high heat.

When you see the oil shimmering, reduce the heat to medium and add the onions and 2 tablespoons of salt. Sauté for 10 minutes, until the onions are soft.

Add the vegetarian ground meat and sauté for 5 to 10 minutes or until brown.

Pour the meat mixture onto the bottom of a 9 × 13 nonstick baking pan. Sprinkle the cumin and garlic powder on top of the meat mixture, followed by a layer of corn and 1 tablespoon of salt.

When the potatoes are done, place them on top of the corn mixture, making sure all the corn is covered.

Sprinkle the remaining salt over the potatoes.

Bake uncovered for 20 minutes.

Makes 4 to 6 servings.

Meat
Main
Dishes

Chicken Schnitzel

This is another specialty created by Elana's dad. Although it's fried, the flavor is remarkable. And if you really want to make an impression, put some sliced russet potatoes in the oil after you've finished the chicken for the best French fries you've ever had.

 INGREDIENTS:

½ cup flour
1 teaspoon garlic powder
1 teaspoon onion powder
1–2 extra-large eggs
2 cups seasoned bread crumbs (more if needed)
1 pound boneless, skinless chicken breasts, sliced thinly horizontally
1½ cups vegetable oil

DIRECTIONS:

In a shallow bowl, mix together the flour, garlic powder, and onion powder. This will be the first of three breading stations.

Beat the egg in a shallow bowl. This will be the second breading station. You may need another beaten egg, depending on how much goes on each piece.

In a third shallow bowl or plate, pour out enough bread crumbs to coat all of the chicken; this is the third breading station. You may need to add more bread crumbs as the breading process goes on.

To bread the chicken, dip a piece of chicken into the flour mixture and shake off any excess. Dip the chicken into the egg, coating the entire piece and letting the excess drip off. Finally, dip the chicken into the bread crumbs, making sure the piece is fully covered. Set each piece aside on a plate as you bread the rest.

In a 10- or 12-inch sauté pan, pour the oil ½ inch deep. Heat the oil over medium heat. When the oil is shimmering, place 2 or 3 pieces of chicken in the pan and brown on both sides, about 5 minutes.

Cut into the chicken to make sure it is fully cooked. You may want to brown the pieces more or less, depending on your preference.

Makes 6 to 8 servings.

Panko Encrusted Honey Mustard Chicken

We should call this dish "surprise chicken" because you'll never guess that there's honey mustard in it until you take a bite (unless you know the name, of course).

 INGREDIENTS:

1 cup flour
¼ cup yellow mustard
½ cup honey
2 cups Panko bread crumbs
1 pound boneless, skinless chicken breasts, sliced thinly horizontally
Extra-virgin olive oil

DIRECTIONS:

Preheat the oven to 400 degrees.

Put the flour in a shallow bowl. This will be the first of three breading stations.

Place the honey and mustard in a shallow bowl and whisk them together. This will be the second breading station.

In a third shallow bowl, pour the Panko bread crumbs. This is the third breading station.

To bread the chicken, dip a piece of chicken into the flour and shake off any excess. Dip the chicken into the honey-mustard mixture, coating the entire piece. Finally, dip the chicken into the bread crumbs, making sure the piece is fully covered. Set each piece aside on a plate as you bread the rest.

Pour about 3 tablespoons of olive oil on a large cookie sheet and spread the oil evenly.

Place the chicken on the cookie sheet, making sure that none of the pieces overlap. (Use two cookie sheets if needed.)

Bake for 10 to 15 minutes per side, until the chicken is golden brown.

Makes 6 to 8 servings.

Pistachio Chicken

We think pistachio nuts are addictive. We also love schnitzel (our recipe is on p. 89). So here's a way to get the best of both worlds without having to face a big vat of oil.

 INGREDIENTS:

1 cup flour
1–2 extra-large eggs, beaten
2 cups pistachio nuts, shelled and finely ground
2 cups Panko bread crumbs
1 pound boneless, skinless chicken breasts, sliced thinly horizontally
1½ cups extra-virgin olive oil

DIRECTIONS:

Preheat the oven to 400 degrees.

For breading, take out three wide, flat bowls. Place the flour into the first bowl, the egg into the second, and the ground pistachios and bread crumbs into the third. Mix the pistachios and bread crumbs together.

To bread the chicken, dip a piece of chicken into the flour and shake off any excess. Dip the chicken into the egg, coating the entire piece. Finally, dip the chicken into the bread crumb mixture, making sure the piece is fully covered. Set each piece aside on a plate as you bread the rest.

Pour the olive oil into the bottom of a 9 × 13 nonstick baking pan. (You may need more than one pan.) Place all of the chicken into the pan and bake for about 10 minutes.

Flip the chicken and bake for an additional 5 to 10 minutes, until the chicken is cooked through.

Makes 6 to 8 servings.

PASSOVER FRIENDLY TIPS:

Use matzah cake meal instead of flour, and use Passover bread crumbs instead of Panko bread crumbs.

Arroz Con Pollo

A taste of Spain on a plate. Our version is based on the traditional method and combines the best features of paella and a slow-cooked chicken dish. And we've simplified the process for you, too.

INGREDIENTS:

1 tablespoon extra-virgin olive oil
1 pound chicken thighs, cut up
2 yellow onions, diced
1 teaspoon kosher salt
1 red bell pepper, chopped
3 cloves garlic, minced
1 (15.4-ounce) can diced tomatoes
1 (6-ounce) can tomato paste
2 cups vegetable stock
3–4 strands saffron
2 teaspoons dried oregano
1 cup arborio rice

 DIRECTIONS:

Pour the oil into a very large skillet with a cover. Set the skillet over high heat. When you see the oil shimmering, reduce the heat to medium.

Pat the chicken dry and place it in the skillet. Brown the chicken, flipping halfway through to brown on both sides, about 8 minutes in all. Remove the chicken from the skillet.

Add the onion to the pan and sauté. Add 1 teaspoon of salt. Stir occasionally, until the onions are soft.

Add the bell pepper and sauté until it starts to soften, about 3 minutes.

Add the garlic and sauté for another 2 to 3 minutes.

Add the diced tomatoes, tomato paste, vegetable stock, saffron, and oregano. Mix well. Bring to a boil, reduce the heat, and simmer for about 5 minutes.

Stir in the rice. Add the chicken back into the skillet in an even layer.

Simmer, covered, on low heat for 30 to 35 minutes, until the chicken and rice have cooked through.

Makes 4 to 6 servings.

Honey Teriyaki Chicken

We've always loved thick teriyaki sauce. Here's a way for you to enjoy it too.

INGREDIENTS:

1 pound boneless, skinless chicken breasts
½ cup honey
¼ cup low-sodium teriyaki sauce

DIRECTIONS:

In a small bowl, mix the honey and teriyaki sauce to create the marinade. Space out the chicken in a 9 × 13 nonstick baking pan and pour the marinade over the chicken. Make sure the chicken is coated well.

Cover the pan with aluminum foil. Place the pan in the refrigerator for a minimum of 1 hour to marinate the chicken.

Preheat the oven to 350 degrees.

Remove the pan from the refrigerator and let it sit for 5 minutes.

Remove the aluminum foil and bake the chicken for 20 to 30 minutes.

Makes 4 to 6 servings.

Sweet and Sour Chicken

We based this recipe on one created by Elana's cousin, Sara Kublin. It's another great way to enjoy Chinese food at home.

 INGREDIENTS:

3 teaspoons vegetable oil
1 large onion, sliced into ½-inch pieces
2 teaspoons kosher salt
1 red bell pepper, sliced into ½-inch pieces
1 pound boneless, skinless chicken breasts, cubed
3 cloves garlic, minced

Sauce:
¾ cup ketchup
½ cup brown sugar
½ cup soy sauce
2 tablespoons white vinegar

DIRECTIONS:

In a small bowl, combine the sauce ingredients. Mix thoroughly and set aside.

Pour the oil into a 10- or 12-inch high-sided pan over high heat. When you see the oil shimmering, add the onions and 1 teaspoon of salt and reduce the heat to medium. Sauté the onions until they have softened, 5 to 10 minutes.

Add the bell pepper and the remaining 1 teaspoon of salt. Sauté for 10 to 15 minutes, until the vegetables are very soft and nearly caramelized.

Add the chicken and stir constantly for 3 to 5 minutes, flipping the pieces of chicken halfway through.

Add the garlic and stir for 1 minute. Reduce the heat to medium-low and add the sauce.

Cook for 5 to 10 more minutes to let the sauce bubble and thicken more.

Serve the chicken by itself or with rice or noodles.

Makes 2 to 4 servings.

Asian Chicken

Elana's mom, Charna Milstein, has a master's degree in Asian chicken salad from nearly every restaurant she's ever visited. We promised her that we'd put a recipe for the dish in the cookbook. And we did one better: this can be served hot for a Chinese food night or cold for a salad a la Charna.

INGREDIENTS

1 teaspoon vegetable oil
1 pound boneless, skinless chicken breasts, cubed

Sauce:
¼ cup sesame seeds
2 tablespoons sesame oil
1 tablespoon vegetable oil
½ cup soy sauce
½ cup light rice vinegar
6 cloves garlic, minced
¼ cup sugar

Corn starch solution:
1 teaspoon corn starch
2 tablespoons water

 ## DIRECTIONS:

Mix the sauce ingredients in a bowl and set aside. In another bowl, mix the corn starch solution ingredients together.

Pour the 1 teaspoon vegetable oil into a 10- or 12-inch high-sided pan over high heat. When you see the oil shimmering, reduce the heat to medium and add the chicken.

Sauté until the chicken is white on nearly every side, flipping the pieces halfway through. Reduce the heat to medium-low and pour the sauce into the pan.

The sauce should come to a boil in about 5 minutes. At that point, add the corn starch solution. Stir until the sauce thickens, about 5 more minutes.

To make this as a salad, let the chicken cool, slice it, and then add it to your favorite set of salad ingredients, spooning on the sauce as a dressing.

Makes 2 to 4 servings.

Wicked Good Baked Chicken

This recipe is an ode to all of our friends in New England, especially Sarah Scarchilli-Janus and Mat Janus, who loved this dish when they came to visit us.

INGREDIENTS:

1 medium yellow onion, sliced into small strips
3–4 cloves garlic, minced
2 whole cloves garlic, peeled
¼ cup (or more, as needed) extra-virgin olive oil
About 1 pound chicken, skin on, cut up
2 tablespoons dried rosemary, chopped
Paprika, to taste

DIRECTIONS:

Preheat the oven to 375 degrees.

Place half of the onion and the 2 whole garlic cloves onto the bottom of a 9 × 13 nonstick baking pan.

Using your hands, spread some of the olive oil and minced garlic under the skin of each piece of chicken. Coat each piece well with more olive oil and minced garlic, the rest of the onions, the rosemary, and the paprika.

Bake uncovered for 30 to 40 minutes.

Makes 2 to 4 servings.

Passover Friendly

Roasted Herb Chicken

This is a great (and cost-effective) way to feed a crowd for a Shabbat or holiday meal. Plus, you'll be reminded of Thanksgiving. Not a bad way to go.

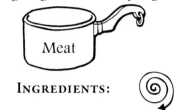

INGREDIENTS:

6 cloves garlic, minced
2 sprigs fresh rosemary, chopped
1 stick margarine, softened
3 medium yellow onions, sliced into small strips
1 (6-ounce) bag baby carrots
1 whole chicken (about 3 pounds), skin on
2 tablespoons extra-virgin olive oil

 DIRECTIONS:

Preheat the oven to 375 degrees.

Mix the rosemary and garlic into the softened margarine.

Coat the bottom of a nonstick 9 × 13 baking pan with olive oil.

Place the onions and carrots into the bottom the pan.

Using your hands, spread the herbed margarine under the skin of the chicken. On top of each piece, spread the rest of the margarine mix, making sure to coat every surface of the chicken.

Bake uncovered for about 30 minutes. Check the internal temperature to make sure it is done. Let the chicken rest for 10 minutes before carving and serving.

Makes 4 to 6 servings.

Passover Friendly

Baked Lemon Chicken

The citrus adds a nice zing to the chicken. This is a nice change from a basic baked chicken.

 INGREDIENTS:

1 tablespoon dried oregano
5 cloves garlic, minced
1 stick margarine, softened
1 teaspoon extra-virgin olive oil
2 medium yellow onions, sliced into small strips
1–2 lemons, sliced
1 pound chicken, skin on, cut up

DIRECTIONS:

Preheat the oven to 375 degrees.

Mix the oregano and garlic into the softened margarine.

Coat the bottom of a 9 × 13 nonstick baking pan with the olive oil. Place all the onions and half of the lemon slices into the pan. Using your hands, spread the herbed margarine under the skin of the chicken. Place a slice of lemon underneath the skin.

On top of each piece of chicken, spread the rest of the herbed margarine along with the onions and a lemon slice. Place the chicken into the pan. (If you have extra lemon slices, spread them around the pan.)

Bake uncovered for about 30 minutes.

Make sure to remove the lemon slices from underneath the skin before serving.

Makes 4 to 6 servings.

Passover Friendly

Balsamic Chicken

This is the epitome of a quick, elegant weeknight meal.

INGREDIENTS:

1 pound boneless, skinless chicken breasts, cut into small strips
1 cup flour
1 (8-ounce) package crimini mushrooms, thinly sliced
3 teaspoons extra-virgin olive oil

Sauce:
⅓ cup balsamic vinegar
6 tablespoons brown sugar

 ## DIRECTIONS:

Whisk the sauce ingredients in a bowl and set aside.

Pat the chicken dry.

Pour the flour into a medium, flat bowl. Dip each piece of chicken in the flour to coat the chicken, shaking off any excess flour.

Pour 2 teaspoons of the olive oil into a 10- or 12-inch high-sided pan over high heat. When you see the oil shimmering, lower the heat to medium and add the chicken. Sauté until the chicken is mostly done, flipping the pieces halfway through.

Reduce the heat to medium-low. Add the mushrooms along with the remaining teaspoon of olive oil.

Sauté the mushrooms for about 2 minutes, making sure to move the chicken so the mushrooms are in direct contact with the pan.

Reduce the heat to low and add the sauce. Cook for about 5 minutes.

Makes 2 to 4 servings.

PASSOVER FRIENDLY TIP:

Use matzah cake meal instead of flour.

Slow Cooker Garlic Chicken

After spending the day in the slow cooker, the chicken falls off the bone and shares its juices with the potatoes. Your mouth should water just reading that sentence.

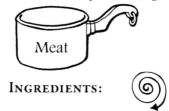

Meat

INGREDIENTS:

2 tablespoons extra-virgin olive oil
1½ pounds red potatoes, quartered
1 large or 2 medium yellow onions, sliced
6 whole garlic cloves, peeled
6 garlic cloves, minced
1 pound chicken, skin on, cut up
1 stick unsalted margarine, softened
2 tablespoons dried rosemary
1 tablespoon dried thyme

 DIRECTIONS:

Sprinkle the olive oil on the bottom of a 6-quart slow cooker.

Spread the potatoes, the whole garlic cloves, and half of the onions onto the bottom of slow cooker, stirring to coat them with the olive oil. Place the chicken into the slow cooker on top of the potatoes, onions, and whole garlic.

Mix the margarine, minced garlic, and herbs together to form a paste. Using your hands, spread the margarine mixture under the skin of the chicken as well on the exterior of each piece of chicken.

Top with the rest of the onions.

Cook on low for 6 to 8 hours, basting every hour if possible.

Makes 4 to 6 servings.

Passover Friendly

Roasted Herb Turkey

Don't let a large bird scare you away from making turkey on Thanksgiving. It might take a while to cook, but the meat will be moist and the herbs will make your guests wonder where you went to culinary school.

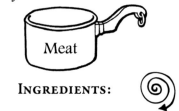

INGREDIENTS:

2 sprigs fresh rosemary, stalks removed, chopped
6 cloves garlic, minced
2 sticks unsalted margarine, softened
2 tablespoons extra-virgin olive oil
3 medium yellow onions, sliced into small strips
1 (6-ounce) bag baby carrots
1 fresh 14-pound turkey

Cavity stuffing:
1 medium yellow onion, cut in half
2 whole cloves garlic, peeled
1 lemon, sliced in half
1 sprig fresh rosemary

 DIRECTIONS:

Preheat the oven to 500 degrees.

Mix the rosemary and minced garlic into the softened margarine to form a paste.

Coat the rack and bottom of a dark metal turkey roasting pan with olive oil. Place the onions and carrots into the bottom the pan.

Place the turkey on the rack and fill the cavity with the onion, whole garlic cloves, lemon, and rosemary. Tie the legs together with kitchen twine.

Using your hands, spread the herbed margarine under the skin of the turkey. On top of the turkey, spread the rest of the herbed margarine, making sure to coat every surface of the turkey.

Bake for about 30 minutes. Cover the breasts with aluminum foil (you can use a toothpick to pin the foil in place). Then reduce the heat to 350 degrees and cook for another 3 to 4 hours, basting the turkey every hour.

Check the internal temperature using a meat thermometer. When the dark meat reaches 165 degrees, remove the turkey from the oven. Let it rest, still covered, for about 10 minutes. Remove the items from the cavity, then carve the turkey and serve.

Makes 6 to 8 servings.

Passover Friendly

Barbecue Turkey Loaf

Meatloaf is boring. We know that. But this all-turkey version is brightened by barbecue sauce, and you won't even need a grill.

Well received 6/15

I doubled recipe & used only 1 env. soup mix as I had regular

Meat

INGREDIENTS:

1 pound ground turkey
1 envelope reduced-sodium dried onion soup mix
¼ cup matzah meal
¼ cup honey barbecue sauce
1 extra-large egg

 ## DIRECTIONS:

Preheat the oven to 350 degrees.

Combine all ingredients in a bowl and mix well.

Place the meat in a nonstick loaf pan, making sure the meat is evenly distributed throughout the pan.

Optional: pour another ⅓ cup of the honey barbecue sauce on top of the loaf.

Bake for 40 minutes.

Makes 4 servings.

PASSOVER FRIENDLY TIP:

Use Passover barbecue sauce.

Slow Cooker Beef Stew

On those cold winter nights, what's better than a stick-to-your-ribs-good dish that didn't take a lot of fuss?

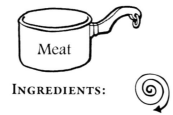

INGREDIENTS:

1½ to 2 pounds beef for stew, cubed
2 large or 3 medium yellow onions, diced
3 large white button mushrooms, sliced
2 red bell peppers, sliced into 1-inch strips
1 (14.5-ounce) can diced tomatoes with liquid
1 (6-ounce) can tomato paste
1 teaspoon kosher salt
1½ tablespoons garlic powder
1 tablespoon chili powder
3 cups vegetable stock

 DIRECTIONS:

Place the beef on the bottom of slow cooker. Add the onions, mushrooms, and bell peppers.

Next, add the tomatoes and tomato paste.

Finally, add the vegetable stock and spices and stir well. Cook on low for 8 to 10 hours.

If possible, taste the stew midway through the cooking time and adjust the salt or spices as needed.

Makes 4 to 6 servings.

PASSOVER FRIENDLY TIP:

If you can't find vegetable stock in a carton, make some using vegetable powder and water.

Grandma Marian's Meatballs

This was Rob's most requested food when he visited his maternal grandmother, Marian Gitlitz, for dinner as a kid. Rob's mom kept the recipe alive, and we've added our own spin to pass along.

 INGREDIENTS:

1 (28-ounce) can tomato sauce
1 (15-ounce) can tomato sauce
1 large yellow onion, chopped
3 cups water (for sauce)
1 tablespoon dried oregano
2 (16-ounce) cans whole cranberry sauce
1 large red bell pepper, chopped
2½ pounds ground turkey (dark meat)
¼ cup old-fashioned oats
1 cup water (for meatballs)
1 tablespoon onion powder
1 tablespoon garlic powder

DIRECTIONS:

To make the sauce, combine the tomato sauce, onions, peppers, 3 cups of water, oregano, and cranberry sauce in a saucepan. Cook on low to medium heat until the mixture is well blended or until you finished forming the meatballs.

To make the meatballs, put the turkey into a bowl and add the oats. Combine well with your hands. Add 1 cup of water, the garlic powder, and the onion powder and combine with your hands again.

Form balls by taking about a tablespoon of the meat mixture and rolling it in your hands.

Add each ball to the sauce. Cover and cook for 3 hours on low to medium heat.

Let the cooked meatballs cool. Refrigerate them overnight to let the flavors meld even more.

Before serving, warm up the sauce and meatballs on low heat for up to an hour, until everything is hot.

Serve the meatballs alone or with rice or pasta.

Makes 6 to 8 servings.

PASSOVER FRIENDLY TIP:

Use matzah meal instead of oats.

Brisket

Since some people in our family don't eat turkey (we'll omit names to protect the guilty), this dish has become almost as important to Thanksgiving as the poultry. But you can enjoy it whenever you want.

 INGREDIENTS:

4 pounds brisket
2 envelopes reduced-sodium dried onion soup mix
3 (16-ounce) cans jellied cranberry sauce

DIRECTIONS:

Preheat the oven to 400 degrees.

Take two generous sheets of heavy-duty aluminum foil and cross-section with another two sheets. Place the sheets in a large disposable roasting pan.

In a bowl, mix the cranberry sauce and onion soup together. Place half of the mixture on the aluminum foil that is in the roasting pan. Then add the meat and place the remaining sauce on top of the meat. Repeat the aluminum foil wrapping procedure on top of the meat, tightly wrapping the meat in the aluminum foil. Add two more sheets of foil so that the meat is completely wrapped. Repeat the wrapping procedure one more time. The more tightly you wrap the meat, the more tender it will become.

Put in oven for at least 4 hours and up to 6. (You really can't overcook the meat, which will fall apart the longer it cooks.)

Makes 4 to 6 servings.

Passover Friendly

Desserts

Chocolate Sandwich Cookie Cake

The blend of a moist yellow cake and crumbled cookies creates a fine crumb to enjoy.
You can find the pareve version of the chocolate sandwich cookies at your local kosher
grocery store.

Pareve

INGREDIENTS:

2 cups unbleached all-purpose flour
1 teaspoon table salt
2 teaspoons baking powder
¾ cup soy milk
1 box instant vanilla pudding
1 cup vegetable shortening
1 cup granulated sugar
2 extra-large eggs
1 teaspoon vanilla extract
Baking spray that contains flour
7 pareve chocolate sandwich cookies, crushed

Icing:
1 cup confectioners' sugar
1–2 tablespoons water
4 pareve chocolate sandwich cookies, crushed

 DIRECTIONS:

Preheat the oven to 350 degrees.

In a bowl, mix the flour, salt, and baking powder.

In another bowl, mix the soy milk and the vanilla pudding.

In a third bowl, cream together the vegetable shortening and sugar, using an electric hand mixer. Then add the eggs and vanilla extract and mix again.

Alternately, add half of the dry ingredients and half of the pudding mixture to the wet ingredients, mixing well with a hand mixer after each addition. Repeat with the remaining dry ingredients and pudding mixture.

Spray a Bundt pan with baking spray. The batter will be very thick, so you will need to use a spoon to pour half of it into the Bundt pan. Then sprinkle the 7 crushed cookies over the bottom half. Spoon the rest of the batter into Bundt pan. Make sure to spread the batter evenly.

Bake for 45 to 50 minutes. Let the cake cool for 30 minutes. Turn the cake over onto a plate.

To make the icing:

In a bowl, whisk together the confectioners' sugar and 1 tablespoon of water. If the mixture is too thick, add a bit more water. You want the mixture to absorb all the confectioners' sugar and be able to be drizzled over the cake without being runny. Drizzle the icing onto the cake and sprinkle the 4 crushed cookies on top.

Makes 12 servings.

Pistachio Chocolate Cake

A Milstein family recipe, this cake contains more chocolate than pistachios. We guarantee that, once you make it, you'll be addicted to this moist, succulent cake.

Pareve

 INGREDIENTS:

1 (18.25-ounce) box yellow or white cake mix
1 (3.4-ounce) package instant pistachio pudding
4 extra-large eggs
1 cup water
¾ cup oil
1 cup chocolate-flavored syrup
3–4 drops green food coloring
Baking spray that contains flour

Icing:
1 tablespoon water
1 cup confectioners' sugar

 DIRECTIONS:

Preheat the oven to 350 degrees.

Combine the cake mix, pudding, eggs, water, and oil in a bowl, using a hand mixer to blend the ingredients thoroughly.

Add the green food coloring to the mixture. (The more drops you add, the greener the batter will be.)

Spray a Bundt pan with baking spray.

Pour three-quarters of the batter into the Bundt pan.

Add the chocolate-flavored syrup to the remaining batter. Pour the chocolate syrup batter into the Bundt pan.

Bake for 50 minutes or until a toothpick inserted into the cake comes out clean.

Allow the cake to cool. Turn it upside down onto a plate.

For the icing, whisk together the water and confectioners' sugar. The icing should be thick and can be poured over the cake.

Makes 12 servings.

German Chocolate Cake

Unfortunately, we can't pass along the recipe to you the way Elana got it: on a small paper plate after a Clark University alumni women's volleyball game. Nevertheless, this simple dessert is quite elegant and will wow anybody who takes a bite.

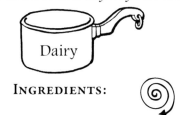

Dairy

 INGREDIENTS:

1 (18.25-ounce) box yellow cake mix
4 extra-large eggs
1 (3.4-ounce) package vanilla instant pudding
⅔ cup vegetable oil
1 cup water
1 cup semisweet chocolate chips
1 bar German chocolate, grated, divided in half
½ cup confectioners' sugar
Baking spray that contains flour

DIRECTIONS:

Preheat the oven to 350 degrees.

Using a hand mixer, combine the cake mix, eggs, pudding, oil, and water on medium speed for 5 minutes. Pour half of the grated chocolate bar into the batter along with the chocolate chips.

Spray a 9 × 13 nonstick baking pan with baking spray. Pour the batter into the pan and bake for 40 to 50 minutes, or until a toothpick inserted into the cake comes out clean.

Remove the cake from the oven and let it sit for 5 minutes.

To make the icing, mix the confectioners' sugar with the remaining grated chocolate and sprinkle it onto the cake.

Makes 12 servings.

Grandma Marian's Apple Cake

We're lucky that Grandma Marian wrote down this recipe before she died. In true family tradition, the original recipe was a list of ingredients with no title or directions at all. We've clarified things for you and the result is truly scrumptious.

Pareve

 INGREDIENTS:

2 apples, peeled, cored, and finely diced
½ cup granulated sugar
¼ cup vegetable oil
1 cup unbleached all-purpose flour
1 teaspoon cinnamon
1 teaspoon baking soda
¼ teaspoon table salt
1 teaspoon vanilla extract
Baking spray that contains flour
1 extra large egg

DIRECTIONS:

Preheat the oven to 350 degrees.

Place the diced apples into a mixing bowl and add the sugar on top. Pour in the oil and egg and stir.

Sift the flour into the apple mixture. Add the baking soda, cinnamon, salt, and vanilla. Mix well.

Spray an 8 × 8 nonstick baking pan with baking spray. Pour the batter into the pan.

Bake for 20 to 25 minutes. Test with a toothpick to make sure the cake is fully cooked.

Makes 2 to 4 servings.

Baked Apple Crisp

Another contribution from Grandma Marian, this recipe perhaps epitomizes what an apple crisp should contain: gooey, caramelized fruit underneath a sweet, crunchy crust. And it's really easy to make, too.

INGREDIENTS:

4–5 small apples, peeled, cored, and sliced thinly
½ cup lemon juice
1 tablespoon margarine for greasing pan
1 tablespoon ground cinnamon
½ cup brown sugar
Additional 5–6 tablespoons unsalted margarine, melted
1 cup unbleached all-purpose flour
1 cup granulated sugar
1 teaspoon baking powder
½ teaspoon table salt

DIRECTIONS:

Preheat the oven to 350 degrees.

As you slice the apples, place them in a bowl with the lemon juice to prevent browning.

Grease a 9 × 9 nonstick baking pan with the 1 tablespoon of margarine.

Layer the sliced apples in the pan.

Combine the cinnamon and brown sugar in a small bowl. Make sure the mixture is well combined and then sprinkle it over the sliced apples.

Melt the 5-6 tablespoons of margarine in a small bowl in the microwave (about 30 seconds).

In a large bowl, combine the flour, sugar, baking powder, and salt.

Add the melted margarine to the flour mixture and combine. The mixture should be crumbly and not too wet.

Sprinkle this mixture over the cinnamon-sugar layer and then bake for 45 minutes.

Let cool 5 minutes and serve warm.

Makes 2 to 4 servings.

Sin Cake

The cake gets its name from the main ingredient (cinnamon) and that fact that it's sinfully delicious. It's our version of a cake that Elana ate quite frequently in her youth.

 INGREDIENTS:

2½ cups unbleached all-purpose flour
1 teaspoon baking soda
3 teaspoons baking powder
1 cup vegetable shortening
1 cup granulated sugar
3 extra-large eggs, beaten
1 cup sour cream (nonfat or pareve)
1 teaspoon vanilla extract
Baking spray that contains flour

Filling:
¾ cup brown sugar
1 tablespoon cinnamon
Chopped nuts (optional)

DIRECTIONS:

Preheat the oven to 350 degrees.

Combine the filling ingredients together. Set aside.

In a small bowl, combine the flour, baking soda, and baking powder. Mix well.

In a large bowl, blend the shortening and sugar and add the eggs. Add half of the dry ingredients and half of the sour cream to the shortening mixture and mix well.

Repeat with the other half of the dry ingredients and the other half of the sour cream. Then add the vanilla and mix again.

Spray a Bundt pan with baking spray.

Pour half of the batter into the Bundt pan. Sprinkle the filling on top.

Pour the remaining batter into the pan. Smooth the batter with the back of a spoon or spatula.

Bake for 1 hour or until a toothpick comes out clean.

Makes 12 servings.

Cinnamon Sugar Mandel Bread (Biscotti)

Straight from the old country, here's a (slightly altered) Grandma Marian recipe that combines the best of traditional mandel bread and biscotti. The cinnamon puts it over the top.

Pareve

INGREDIENTS:

Parchment paper
2 cups unbleached all-purpose flour
1 teaspoon baking powder
¼ teaspoon table salt
2 teaspoons ground cinnamon
1 heaping tablespoon solid vegetable shortening
¾ cup granulated sugar
2 extra-large eggs

Topping:
1 teaspoon ground cinnamon
½ cup granulated sugar

 ## DIRECTIONS:

Preheat the oven to 350 degrees.

Line two cookie sheets with parchment paper.

In a small bowl, combine the flour, baking powder, salt, and cinnamon.

In a large bowl, cream together the vegetable shortening and the sugar. Add the eggs and beat the mixture together. Stir in the flour mixture.

On a floured surface, divide the dough into halves. Shape each half into a log, 6 to 8 inches long and no more than ¾ inch thick. Transfer the logs to the prepared cookie sheets.

Bake for 20 minutes and let cool for 15 minutes.

With a spray bottle filled with room-temperature water, spray the logs thoroughly.

Slice the logs into ¾-inch strips and lay each slice on its side.

Sprinkle each piece with cinnamon sugar and put the cookies back in the oven for another 15 minutes.

Makes 20 cookies.

Cookie Cutter Sugar Cookies

Our friend Stew Bromberg got a hamantaschen recipe from the JCC where he worked in Massachusetts. We made some tweaks and turned it into something so easy that you'll never make sugar cookies from a mix again.

Pareve

 INGREDIENTS:

2½ cups unbleached all-purpose flour
2 teaspoons baking powder
1 teaspoon table salt
1 stick unsalted margarine, softened
1½ cups granulated sugar
2 extra-large eggs
1 teaspoon vanilla extract

DIRECTIONS:

Preheat the oven to 350 degrees.

In a small bowl, mix together the flour, baking powder, and salt.

In a large bowl, cream together the softened margarine and sugar, using an electric hand mixer if desired. Beat in the eggs and vanilla extract.

Add half of the dry ingredients into the margarine mixture and mix well. Add the other half and mix again. The batter will be very sticky.

Divide the dough in halves and roll each half into a ball. Place each ball in a separate piece of plastic wrap and refrigerate for at least 2 hours (overnight would be best).

Take out one of the dough balls and place it on a floured board or piece of parchment paper.

Using a floured rolling pin, roll out the dough to be no more than ⅛ inch to ¼ inch thick.

Using whatever shape cookie cutters you like, cut out the dough and place the shapes on ungreased cookie sheets. Put the cookie sheets back in the refrigerator for 15 minutes. This is to help the cookies retain their shape when baking (so they don't spread out).

Bake for 10 to 12 minutes.

Makes 30 to 40 cookies, depending on the cookie cutters used.

Milstein Family Fruit Salad

You'll be a convert, too, after making fruit salad the Milstein way. The strawberry jam and orange juice create a tasty gravy that only gets better with time.

Pareve

 INGREDIENTS:

2 red delicious apples, cored and diced

2 oranges, peeled and diced

1½ pounds grapes (green or red or both), washed and separated (as many as you want to add)

1 whole pineapple, top, core, and skin removed, sliced lengthwise into 4 sections, juice reserved

1 pint strawberries, green tops removed and quartered

1 cup strawberry preserves

1 cup orange juice (from a carton)

DIRECTIONS:

Place all fruit in a big bowl.

Add the reserved pineapple juice, orange juice, and jam. Mix well.

Makes 12 servings.

PASSOVER FRIENDLY TIP:

Use kosher for Passover preserves.

Palmeras Con Chocolate

During a trip to Segovia, Spain, we were wandering around the town where Elana spent her semester abroad in college. Elana remembered a bakery on the corner of the street where she used to live and ate these treats all the time. We finally had the opportunity to share this experience together.

Dairy/
Pareve

 INGREDIENTS:

2 sheets pareve puff pastry, defrosted
At least 4 cups granulated sugar (use as needed)
½ cup semisweet chocolate chips
1 heaping tablespoon vegetable shortening

DIRECTIONS:

Preheat the oven to 375 degrees.

Unfold 1 piece of the puff pastry on a piece of parchment paper covered with sugar.

Cover the top of the puff pastry with sugar evenly.

Fold the sides of the rectangle toward the center so they meet exactly at the middle of the dough. Again, cover the top with sugar.

Fold one side of the dough over the other, so it appears to be a log. You will have 4 layers.

Slice the log into 18 to 20 equal pieces. As you slice, make sure each piece is thoroughly coated with sugar on all sides.

There will be leftover sugar on the parchment paper. Lay the slices, cut side up, onto two baking sheets.

Bake the cookies for 6 to 8 minutes. Flip them over and bake for another 5 or 6 minutes until golden brown on each side.

Place the cookies on parchment paper to cool.

Repeat the entire process with the other sheet of puff pastry.

Combine the chocolate chips and vegetable shortening in a microwave-safe bowl. Heat the mixture on high for 1 minute and stir to combine.

Dip the tip of each cooled cookie into the melted chocolate and place it back on the parchment paper for the chocolate to harden.

Makes about 40 cookies.

Passover Jam Bars

This Passover-friendly dessert was shared with us by Elana's good friend and colleague, Ronnie Oppenheim. This twist on a Linzer torte will have you amazed that there's no flour involved.

Pareve

INGREDIENTS:

Crust:
1 stick unsalted margarine, softened
1 egg yolk
Pinch salt
½ cup granulated sugar
1 cup sifted matzah cake meal

Filling:
¾ cup Passover preserves, any flavor

 DIRECTIONS:

Preheat the oven to 325 degrees.

In a large bowl, combine the crust ingredients.

Spread ¾ of the dough into the bottom of an 8 × 8 nonstick baking pan. Bake for 20 minutes.

Refrigerate the remaining dough.

When the crust has baked, spread the preserves on top of the crust and crumble the remaining dough on top of the preserves.

Bake for another 30 minutes.

The recipe can be doubled and baked in a 9 × 13 nonstick baking pan. If you double the recipe, you can use a different preserve topping on each side.

Makes 4 to 6 servings.

Passover Friendly

Passover Chocolate Swirl Cake

Desperate for a change from yet another boring Passover yellow cake, we started adding different things. This was the most successful result.

 INGREDIENTS:

2 boxes Passover yellow cake mix
6 extra-large eggs
1 cup oil
1 box vanilla pudding mix
¼ cup water
1 cup chocolate-flavored syrup
Nonstick cooking spray or margarine, as needed

DIRECTIONS:

Preheat the oven to 350 degrees.

Grease a 9 × 13 nonstick baking pan generously with nonstick cooking spray or margarine.

Using a hand mixer, blend the cake mix, egg, oil, pudding mix, and water in a large bowl.

Pour half of the batter into the pan.

Add the chocolate-flavored syrup to the rest of the batter and add it to the pan.

Bake for 60 to 90 minutes, until a toothpick comes out clean.

Add icing if desired. (For recipe and instructions, see p. 121-122.)

Makes 8 to 10 servings.

Passover Friendly

Glossary of Cooking/Baking Terms

Baste: To pour liquid (usually taken from the pan where the food is cooking) over the top of food at certain times.

Caramelize: For our purposes, to cook vegetables until they are soft and the sugars inside them have caused the food to turn brown.

Chop: To cut food into either small or large pieces.

Cream: To combine two items together (usually margarine and sugar) until they form a smooth mixture.

Cube: To cut food into ½-inch squares.

Dice: To cut food into ¼-inch squares.

Grate: To cut food into smaller pieces or thin shreds by rubbing it along a box that has serrated holes for cutting (a box grater).

Marinate: To place food in a seasoned liquid so that the food will absorb flavor and become more tender.

Mince: To chop food into very small pieces.

Roast: To cook a food in an oven in an uncovered vessel so that the food will have a brown exterior.

Sauté: To cook foods quickly in a small amount of fat (such as oil or margarine) over direct heat.

Slice: To cut foods into long, thin strips.

Stir-Fry: To move the foods in a pan around as you fry them, usually over higher heat for a longer time.

Whisk: To incorporate ingredients using a metal wire instrument and not a fork (as for beating).

Index

V

W

About the Authors

Both Elana Milstein and Rob Yunich have been cooking since their youth. *The Kitchen Dance*, their first book, earns its name from their struggle to keep a kosher home in tight quarters—something many people can relate to on a daily basis. From the first time they cooked together, Rob and Elana had to find ways to "dance" around each other in the kitchen, making an effort to learn each other's movements and avoid collisions—all while sticking to recipes and making sure everything was cooked properly. This not only brought them closer together as a couple but made them better chefs.

By day, Elana is a technology coordinator and computer teacher for a local Jewish day school. A Rhode Island native, she has lived in the Washington, D.C., area since 1999.

Rob is a veteran writer, blogger, and communications professional. He has lived in and around the nation's capital for most of his life.

In 2002, after years of playing volleyball exclusively, Elana decided to join a softball team (captained by Rob) and the rest is history. The two immediately began spending time together in and out of the kitchen and were married in 2004.

The Kitchen Dance: A New Take on Kosher Cooking is full of easy-to-understand, foolproof recipes that work perfectly for those who want to cook together or nurture a budding romance. The book earns its name from many people's struggle to keep a kosher home in tight quarters. As the cover drawing illustrates, it's often difficult to "dance" around somebody else in the kitchen while preparing a meal, all while sticking to recipes and making sure everything is cooked properly. If you've been facing this struggle for years, and never seemed to find a cookbook that understood your quandary, worry no more. Whether you need to make dinner after a long day at the office or you want to make a special meal in a flash, this is a cookbook that feels your pain.

The Kitchen Dance includes tips on what to have in the pantry, what equipment you'll need to buy, a guide on how to "dance," a glossary, sample menus, Passover tips, and much more. Notable recipes include:

* Potato and Leek Soup
* Tahina

* Jasmine Rice Pilaf
* Tortilla Española
* Pistachio Chicken
* Sin Cake

If you're a vegetarian, Jewish or not, you'll have plenty of recipes from which to choose. In fact, other than those in chapter 4 (and the chicken soup recipe), every recipe in this book will fit your lifestyle.

Breinigsville, PA USA
03 November 2009
226936BV00002B/1/P

9 781604 943245